"Finally a book on spiritual direction firm. ... ...-
istry of Jesus. In *Soul Guide*, Professor Demarest has fashioned a crown jewel
with many facets to illuminate our spiritual path. If you are serious about your
spiritual journey, you will want to travel with *Soul Guide*."

—Father Andrew Miles, O.S.B., coordinator of The School for
Charismatic Spiritual Directors, Benedictine Monastery, Pecos, NM

"Bruce Demarest skillfully explores how Jesus ministered spiritual direction to
people across the vast spectrum of human need and life. *Soul Guide* will be a
welcome resource for pastors and church leaders interested in guiding others
into deeper intimacy with the triune God."

—Tom Schwanda, associate professor of spiritual formation,
Reformed Bible College (Grand Rapids, MI)

"Once again, Bruce has given us something to nourish our souls and encourage our spirits. Many people have a physical trainer to help them strengthen
their bodies. In over thirty years of Christian living, I've discovered that growing spiritual muscles is a much greater challenge than growing physical muscles. This book is like having a personal spiritual trainer at your fingertips."

—Gary J. Oliver, Th.M., Ph.D., executive director of The Center
for Marriage and Family Studies; professor of psychology and
practical theology, John Brown University

"Using a wise blend of firsthand experience and formation wisdom, classic and
contemporary, the author of this inspiring guide draws us into the heart of
Jesus as the master and minister of care for searching souls. This is a book for
practitioners as well as for ordinary persons wondering how to align themselves
with God's will."

—Susan Muto, Ph.D., dean, Academy of Formative Spirituality;
author of *Meditation in Motion*

"I have found this book to be a solid introduction to the ministry of spiritual
direction. It grounds the ministry of spiritual direction in the life and tradition
of the Christian community, clearly articulates the urgent need for this ministry today, and creatively illustrates the ministry of spiritual direction by inter-
facing contemporary scenarios with Jesus' ministry of spiritual direction to a
diverse variety of persons."

—M. Robert Mulholland, Jr., professor of New Testament,
Asbury Theological Seminary

soulguide

Following Jesus As Spiritual Director

Dr. Bruce Demarest

NAVPRESS

Bringing Truth to Life
P.O. Box 35001, Colorado Springs, Colorado 80935

OUR GUARANTEE TO YOU

We believe so strongly in the message of our books that
we are making this quality guarantee to you. If for any
reason you are disappointed with the content of this
book, return the title page to us with your name and
address and we will refund to you the list price of the
book. To help us serve you better, please briefly describe
why you were disappointed. Mail your refund request to:
NavPress, P.O. Box 35002, Colorado Springs, CO 80935.

The Navigators is an international Christian organization. Our mission is to reach, disciple, and equip people
to know Christ and to make Him known through successive generations. We envision multitudes of diverse
people in the United States and every other nation who have a passionate love for Christ, live a lifestyle of
sharing Christ's love, and multiply spiritual laborers among those without Christ.

NavPress is the publishing ministry of The Navigators. NavPress publications help believers learn biblical
truth and apply what they learn to their lives and ministries. Our mission is to stimulate spiritual formation
among our readers.

Cover design by David Carlson Design
Cover image from Photonica
Creative Team: David Hazard, Greg Clouse, Nat Akin, Pat Miller

Some of the anecdotal illustrations in this book are true to life and are included with the permission of the
persons involved. All other illustrations are composites of real situations, and any resemblance to people living
or dead is coincidental.

Unless otherwise identified, all Scripture quotations in this publication are taken from the HOLY BIBLE:
NEW INTERNATIONAL VERSION® (NIV®). Copyright © 1973, 1978, 1984 by International Bible
Society. Used by permission of Zondervan Publishing House. All rights reserved. Other versions used include:
the *New American Standard Bible* (NASB), © The Lockman Foundation 1960, 1962, 1963, 1968, 1971, 1972,
1973, 1975, 1977; *The Message: New Testament with Psalms and Proverbs* by Eugene H. Peterson, copyright ©
1993, 1994, 1995, used by permission of NavPress Publishing Group; the *New Revised Standard Version*
(NRSV), copyright © 1989, by the Division of Christian Education of the National Council of the Churches
of Christ in the USA, used by permission, all rights reserved; the *Holy Bible, New Living Translation*, (NLT)
copyright © 1996. Used by permission of Tyndale House Publishers, Inc., Wheaton, Illinois 60189. All rights
reserved.

Demarest, Bruce A.
  Soul guide : following Jesus as spiritual director / Bruce Demarest.
      p. cm.
Includes bibliographical references.
  ISBN 1-57683-286-4
  1. Spiritual direction. I. Title.
  BV5053 .D46 2003
  253.5'3--dc21
                                           2003007018

Printed in the United States of America

1 2 3 4 5 6 7 8 9 10 / 07 06 05 04 03

FOR A FREE CATALOG OF
NAVPRESS BOOKS & BIBLE STUDIES,
CALL 1-800-366-7788 (USA)
OR 1-416-499-4615 (CANADA)

Contents

PART 4 / GUIDING OTHERS, JESUS-STYLE

Acknowledgments

GRATITUDE IS DUE, FIRST OF ALL, TO MY LIFELONG PARTNER, ELSIE, FOR her steady encouragement during the writing of this book. I am indebted to Reverend Brad Strait and Dr. Randy MacFarland for reading the manuscript, either in whole or in part, as well as to Reverend Janet Buntrock for providing valuable illustrative material.

I owe a large debt to members past and present of the Pecos Benedictine Monastery and its School for Spiritual Directors for planting the passion seeds for the ministry of spiritual guidance. Likewise to Denver Seminary students, who in courses in spiritual formation and guidance shared their insights into this life-giving ministry.

I am particularly indebted to NavPress senior acquisitions editor Don Simpson for encouraging pursuit of this project, and to developmental editor David Hazard and NavPress project editor Greg Clouse for their uncommon wisdom in facilitating its completion.

Finally, I am grateful also to the faculty, administration, and trustees of Denver Seminary for granting a sabbatical leave that permitted focused attention to this project, which I trust will equip Christian disciples to be more compassionate and effective "shepherds of God's flock" (1 Peter 5:2).

Soli Deo Gloria

Part 1

Soul Care
Yesterday and Today

Jesus, Our Model

THROUGHOUT THE CENTURIES, MINISTRIES OF SPIRITUAL GUIDANCE have been a gift of grace for the people of God. Unfortunately, in some quarters of the church today, the true ministry of spiritual guidance—or spiritual direction, as it has long been known—remains an enigma. Many believers are left struggling with a serious question: How do we live in nourishing communion with an invisible and holy God who is, nonetheless, "with us"? This is a great and often painful mystery for many Christians, as are the questions about living in peaceful community with other people.

Loving God and loving others were indeed Jesus' two most important spiritual directives to us (see Mark 12:29-31). As it happens, these are also the toughest to keep. Who will help us understand how to live in ways that help us grow in spiritual maturity as we seek to fulfill these, our Lord's great commands? Sadly, for many Christians, following the Way of Jesus Christ means little more than weekly church attendance and renewed resolutions at moral living. They experience little in the way of real, individual direction. They feel their souls are not being cared for.

As a result, many Christians today are seeking spiritual direction, and in various ways.

Disciples in Search of Direction

JERRY HAS BEEN a pastor for many years. In the beginning, his ministry felt alive and exciting, and the two churches in which he served both grew. Eventually, though, Jerry became aware that something was absent: He lacked passion for his work. In a short time, he felt drained. Not only was he faltering in his vocation, his relationship with his wife and children became burdensome. He found himself lashing out impatiently at home or withdrawing completely, and feeling ashamed either way.

In his eleventh year of ministry, a sense of anguish, almost despair, had taken hold in Jerry. Any sense of enthusiasm or God's presence was gone. He realized that he hated his work . . . hated his life. Quiet desperation tortured him for months, until he confided his torment to a friend.

At the friend's suggestion, Jerry took a week out of his schedule to visit a retreat center, where he spent time with a spiritual director. The term *spiritual director* was new to Jerry, and at first he was wary. But what he found as he relaxed and opened up was the beginning of substantial healing and renewal.

Mainly, the spiritual director provided godly perspective, listening intently for long periods of time to Jerry's expressions of anguish and to his questions. He asked many questions as well, about Jerry's life, his experiences, his ways of connecting with God—and also about the things that made Jerry feel disconnected from God. Jerry found himself opening up, taking the long view of his own life, and also confiding secrets, doubts, pains, and disappointments he'd never really spoken of to anyone, ever. As the week progressed, the director continually helped Jerry to make sense of great patterns in his life—which he'd never seen before—and to understand them as the great, long outworkings of God's themes and plans for his entire existence. Jerry was able to see not just individual sins and failures—of which he'd been very aware—but also where attitudes and lack of focus had caused him to veer off the path of God's will for him.

When Jerry left the retreat center, he had the great sense that his walk of faith had taken a great turn. The ministry of spiritual direction had helped him begin to deepen and mature in his understanding of God's ways in his life.

Patricia was not so much in search of spiritual direction at the depth that Jerry was. She sensed she needed more particular guidance, because she'd come to what seemed a big fork in the road.

Patricia had married Bill when they were both very young. In short order, they'd had two children. Patricia had become a Christian; Bill had not. As the kids grew, it became painfully obvious that their styles of parenting, and especially disciplining, were at odds. Bill was liberal and lenient; Patricia was conservative and believed in training children to obey their elders without a fight. Very quickly, their parenting clashes led to marital clashes. How could she be an effective parent, Patricia agonized, when Bill bucked her every step of the way? And how could she honor him as her husband, when he made it so difficult by not honoring her desire to raise the children according to her values?

Patricia's immediate need was not for the "big overview" of life, but for specific spiritual guidance in this one situation. And so she sought a biblical counselor to help her work on her parenting and marriage dilemmas.

Joe had been a Christian a long time, and he'd always lived in the same area in the northeast. Then his company was sold, and his job was transferred to the West Coast.

For a long time, Joe felt alone in his new location. He didn't seem able to connect with anyone, even though he attended church, Bible studies, and men's retreats. Then one day he met Frank. Frank was considerably older, and in many ways, on the surface, Joe was probably the last guy Frank would have reached out to as a friend. But Frank took an immediate interest in Joe; he made a point to call him and ask how he was settling into his new job and neighborhood. It was obvious that Frank just *cared* about Joe and his well-being. Frank made it easy for Joe to open up and talk about anything, from feelings of loneliness and displacement, to questions he had about his faith. And every time, Frank had an easy way of turning Joe's attention back to God and His constant care.

"Man," he said to Frank one day, "I've only known you a couple of months—but I feel like I've known you my whole life."

Joe found in Frank what has been called a *soul friend;* that is, someone who will stay at our side through the everyday ups and downs of life, helping us to maintain our faith focus.

Each one of these people experienced a different type of spiritually guiding relationship. Each is valid and necessary, and in the next chapter we'll look more closely at each one. Spiritual counselors and soul friends may be very familiar to us, but it's important for us to recognize how they fit into God's plan for our soul care. What we want to focus on in this chapter is the fact that every one of us has a great hunger within to find deeper meaning and purpose, and a closer, stronger relationship with God. We know we need direction.

To this end, many are visiting monasteries and retreat centers and meeting with spiritual directors in person or on the Internet. For those unfamiliar with the term *spiritual direction,* here is a simple working definition: "Spiritual direction refers to the ministry of soul care in which a gifted and experienced Christian helps another person to grow in relationship with and obedience to God by following the example of Jesus Christ."

Spiritual Direction: A Grace Revived

SPIRITUAL DIRECTION, AND the whole field of spiritual guidance, is enjoying a well-deserved revival in our times. Given the great need for it, this may be a new movement of God's Spirit, as ever more Christian leaders express the need for deep renewal and fresh direction.

An article in *Christianity Today* entitled "From Mass Evangelist to Soul Friend" describes the spiritual journey of evangelist Leighton Ford. After a thirty-year career preaching to large audiences (with the Billy Graham Evangelistic Association), Ford felt the need for sabbatical space, to seek new vision. So he spent the quietness of those uncluttered days reading Annie

Dillard's book *Pilgrim at Tinker Creek* and practicing spiritual disciplines. This was new spiritual territory for Ford but, as he recounts, the benefits he experienced redirected his whole life. Graced with a fresh vision of intimacy with God, Ford traded in the pulpit for the one-on-one ministry of spiritual direction. Ford now spends his time listening to a spiritual seeker's story, pointing him to Christ if needed, and being used of God to deepen his relationship with the Savior. For Ford, "The heart of spiritual direction is helping the other person to listen and pay attention to what God is saying."[1]

Ford's experience, and the similar experiences of many other evangelical Christians, stands as evidence that many are stepping outside the evangelical tradition to explore ancient Christian disciplines and practices that promote spiritual growth and maturity—"new" means to find the soul care and guidance they're looking for. This trend, which is gaining momentum, raises some questions: How does following Jesus Christ, as His disciple, relate to seeking spiritual direction? Isn't our primary relationship with God supposed to be "through" Christ himself, the "one mediator between God and men" (1 Timothy 2:5)?

Jesus Foremost

This book is about Jesus as the model spiritual director for twenty-first-century disciples.

As Christians we confess that Jesus the Christ is the fullness of God, come to us in human flesh to offer us the example of a life lived perfectly under the guidance and direction of God. As such, Jesus Himself is the perfect paradigm for completed humanity and the pattern for Christian ministry. Looking to Jesus as *human beings* we find answers to the questions and issues with which we all struggle. Looking to Jesus as *disciples* we find in Him the perfect pattern of how to minister grace to spiritual seekers.

This book, therefore, has two purposes. The first is to discover what Jesus says to those of us today who are keenly aware of our need for personal spiritual guidance. The second is to draw from the ministry of Jesus principles that will enable us—especially pastors, counselors, and others in the spiritual-care professions—to be effective guides for others. Though Jesus is our main model from which to learn the art of spiritual direction, He isn't our only model.

Along with Jesus, the Bible provides us many helpful examples of men and women who offer insight into the work of spiritual guidance and direction. Moses, Naomi, Nathan, and the apostle Paul stand out as effective spiritual guides. Two thousand years of Christian history also reveal other examples of godly spiritual directors, including the desert masters, Martin Luther, John of the Cross, numerous Puritan divines, John Wesley, as well as contemporaries such as Henri Nouwen, Eugene Peterson, and James Houston. Founders of religious orders—for instance, Bernard of Clairvaux (the Cistercians), Ignatius of Loyola (the Jesuits), and Teresa of Avila (the Carmelites)—have also made important contributions to Christian spiritual direction. In the end, of course, we return to Jesus as our primary model. For while we can learn a good deal from the insights of great human spiritual leaders, the all-wise and compassionate Son of God is our ultimate pattern for receiving and giving spiritual direction.

My personal belief is that it's essential for us to study Jesus' role in the life-giving ministry of spiritual direction. The instruction we get from studying His intentions and methods will be crucial in our own spiritual lives and in the lives of those to whom we offer direction. Why do I believe Jesus' place is central?

First, Jesus made spiritual direction possible by providing the remedy for sin on the cross and launching believers on the spiritual journey to new life in God (see John 10:9). Second, Jesus is the infallible Way to the Father for each pilgrim who sets out on this journey (see John 14:6). Finally, Jesus is the model spiritual director who ministered spiritual guidance to first-century seekers and disciples. Virtually every conversation Jesus had and every teaching He gave offered spiritual guidance. Jesus was always pointing people to God and, if we claim to be His followers, so must we. Remember the Lord's words, "I have set you an example that you should do as I have done for you" (John 13:15). Because Jesus was and is the Lord of Life, we can trust that His ministry of spiritual direction while on earth covered the range of needs and experiences we will face in our varied lives, complex creatures that we are. He focused on primary issues of knowing, being, and doing—constantly directing people to right beliefs, right relationships, and right conduct.

Imitating Jesus

IF WE ARE going to look to Jesus as our model, where do we start?

We begin in part 1 by looking to the Gospels, where we find Jesus "in action." As we watch Him in His encounters with people from all walks of life, and in complex situations, we can begin to comprehend His heart and imitate His practice. Jesus' last words before ascending to heaven apply both to Peter and to us: "You must follow me" (John 21:22)—for when He invited us to follow, He meant it as a directive and not as mere suggestion.

Our purpose, then, is to model our life after His life and our ministry to others after His. The apostle John put it this way: "Whoever claims to live in him must walk as Jesus did" (1 John 2:6). The apostle Paul was also passionate about copying Christ: "Be imitators of me," he wrote, "just as I also am of Christ" (1 Corinthians 11:1, NASB). Paul's word for "imitator" literally means one who "mimics." To follow Christ is to mimic Him. Peter wrote, "Christ suffered for you, leaving you an example, that you should follow in his steps" (1 Peter 2:21). As Christians we trust Christ's merits for salvation, and so also we imitate His example in ministry.

Bernard of Clairvaux (d. 1153) said, "In vain are we called Christians if we live not according to the example and discipline of Christ."[2] Throughout the whole of church history, her leaders have likewise urged the *imitatio Christi* as the way to practice vital faith. The early bishop and theologian Clement of Alexandria (d. 215) wrote: "One truly follows the Savior by arranging everything to be like him,"[3] and Gregory the Great (d. 604) added, "Everything that our blessed Savior wrought in his mortal body he did for our example and instruction."[4] The great medieval theologian Thomas à Kempis (d. 1471) urged, "Imitate Christ in life and behavior. . . . The clue to understanding Christ? Conform one hundred percent to his life."[5] John Arndt (d. 1621), a famed Lutheran pastor, wrote, "If a man loves Christ, he must also love to copy his holy life." Although we fall short of this goal, Arndt wrote, "It is fitting that such a state should be loved, breathed after, and pursued with our utmost efforts."[6] The French spiritual director François Fénelon (d. 1715) emphasized much the same: "We must imitate Jesus. This is to live as he lived, to think as he thought, to conform to his image, which is the seal of our sanctification."[7]

How do we imitate Jesus? How do we follow His pattern for ourselves and in the spiritual guidance we offer others? This may first sound like a goal set too high, or even impossible to reach.

Copying Christ, however, does not mean some kind of clonelike repetition of all Christ's actions. We are not empowered to die for sins or judge the world. To attempt such supernatural works, as Calvin put it, would be to "challenge God to a duel!"[8] Rather, we imitate Christ by sharing the passion of His heart and following the general pattern of His ministry. We begin by reflecting on the spirit, strategy, and style of Jesus' ministry to a variety of people in real-life encounters. We pray that the Spirit may empower us to follow Him as we engage spiritual needs in our own spheres of influence. Thankfully, imitation of Jesus is doable, for the Lord who said, "follow me," and "learn of me," called us to possibilities, not impossibilities.

Our task—to imitate Jesus—reminds me of the story of a budding young painter who desired to create artwork as elegant as that of her teacher, a renowned master of form and color. She painted several scenes, but never felt she attained her teacher's level of excellence. Then she got the bright idea that if she used her teacher's brushes she could paint great art. But she was disappointed. Her paintings still failed to measure up to the instructor's works. Seeing the young woman's struggles, her teacher finally said, "It's not my paintbrushes you need. It's my spirit."

What we ultimately need, if we are going to experience and minister spiritual guidance in the name of Jesus Christ, is a passionate spirit (the Holy Spirit) and the compassionate heart of Jesus. Today, we're enamored of the popular slogan "What would Jesus do?" Perhaps we'd be better off considering the question "What *did* Jesus do?"

In Jesus Christ, then, we find the pattern of spiritual guidance and the qualities of the ideal spiritual director. And as we proceed in this matter of imitating Christ, we'd do well to heed the caution of William Law (d. 1761): "It is as irregular to vary from his example, as it is false to dissent from his doctrines."[9]

In part 2 we will examine the range of Jesus' encounters with a variety of people we meet in the Gospels. From these encounters we'll learn how Jesus ministered spiritual direction to those with concerns and needs that are amazingly similar to our own.

But first, let's take time to look at the wide variety of human needs that both require and benefit from the ministry of spiritual direction.

TRY IT YOURSELF

1. Tapping into the Heart of Jesus

Read straight through Matthew's gospel. As you do, note the various things about which Jesus is passionate, intense, or deliberate. Write out a list of these. Then try your hand at writing a "purpose statement" that focuses the main passions that characterize Jesus' life and ministry into a single goal or intent.

What would you say was the most passionate impulse that beat within the heart of Jesus?

2. An Exercise in Self-Examination

The Reformer, Martin Luther, wrote that believers are called to be "little Christs" to one another and to the world. Take a few moments to reflect quietly on specific ways in which your life reflects the passion and purpose of Jesus Christ. In which ways do you fall short?

Do the same kind of careful reflection, focusing on aspects of your Christian service or ministry.

3. An Honest Assessment

Where do you find you most need the ministry of spiritual direction? Or to put it another way, where do you most need personal soul care?

We *Need* the
Ministry of Soul Care

E VEN A QUICK GLANCE AT EITHER THE BROADER CULTURE OR AT THE church reveals a vast range of serious spiritual needs crying for attention. These are needs that the ministry of spiritual direction can address as maturing believers engage in the soul-caring work of Christ.

What are these needs? Let's consider some of them closely.

Soul Care and the Needs
of the Broader Culture

AMERICA REMAINS A highly religious culture, the most "Christian" nation on earth. A Gallup survey reveals that 96 percent of American adults profess belief in God or a universal spirit. Some 91 percent believe in heaven, while 88 percent call themselves Christians, and 69 percent say they're members of a church, synagogue, or other religious group.[1] Unfortunately, our religious claims are not matched by our day-to-day lives. Concern for America's spiritual state is, in fact, shared by devout people of various faiths.

Recently my wife and I attended a lecture by Jamling Tenzing Norgay, the son of Tenzing Norgay Sherpa, who, with Sir Edmund Hillary in 1953, was the first to climb Mount Everest. Jamling later summited Everest with the 1996 IMAX filming expedition and wrote about the experience in his book, *Touching My Father's Soul*. Jamling attended college in Wisconsin and operates an outdoor adventure business in Jackson Hole, Wyoming, so he's well acquainted with the North American scene. A devout Buddhist, Jamling expresses deep concern at the decline of spiritual vitality in the United States. He writes:

> I assumed that America had become prosperous and developed by virtue of its spiritual progress. But those of us who have visited the country find ourselves asking where that sense of sacredness and spirituality has gone. Its absence, I can understand now, is the source of restlessness, dissatisfaction, and confusion that I

saw afflicting many Americans. Wealth and possessions haven't eased their malaise. Perhaps they have only aggravated it.[2]

Osama bin Laden and his henchmen said they committed the horrific terrorist attacks on New York and Washington on September 11, 2001 because they were angry at America. They claimed to be repulsed by the moral decadence and irreverence of prosperous America and the West. They are angered by what they perceive to be this country's alleged greed, materialism, sexual immorality, and disregard for the world's poor.

Researchers George Barna and Mark Hatch report that America is currently experiencing "moral and spiritual anarchy."[3] For millions of Americans, the faith experience is no longer governed by such values as acceptance of absolutes, reverence for God, and personal holiness. Bible reading, church, and adult Sunday school attendance have decreased over the past decade, and in the area of doctrine, USA TODAY reports that "Most people think the Bible is not totally accurate, Jesus sinned while on earth, and Satan is 'hogwash.'"[4] More than two-thirds of American adults define "success in life" without any reference to spiritual or moral values, but solely in terms of acquiring money, possessions, and status.[5]

Amidst unparalleled prosperity, the American public admits to being deeply, personally lonely. What causes this inner isolation? Such things as the shattering of communal bonds, exhaustion caused by sixty-hour work-weeks, boredom with our consumer culture, feeling owned by possessions and possessed by addictions. We are satiated by sensualism in the media, buried by information, stressed out by labor-saving gadgetry, and depressed by the erosion of transcendent values and hope for the future. A man who in the last year purchased a new pager, cell phone, personal organizer, digital camera, and global positioning device—unable to determine adequately how each worked—wrote to a manufacturer: "Thanks for your latest gizmo, but we haven't figured out the last one."

Three miles from our home stands Columbine High School, tucked into the quiet, middle-class, and otherwise safe enclave of Littleton, Colorado. This is a town dotted with manicured golf courses and crowded churches. In April 1999 two teenagers from professional families entered the school building wearing T-shirts with the word "RAGE" printed on the front. Packing guns and bombs, they proceeded in a several-hour rampage to kill ten other students and one teacher before taking their own lives by bullets to the head. The media widely publicized one of the killer's questions, which he put to a frightened student huddled under a table: "Do you believe in God?" When the student, Cassie Bernall, courageously replied, "I believe in God," he shot her through the head.

The brutality of Columbine—and of other sick and violent acts around the nation—sounds an echo from deep within the soul of our culture. The echo is the gasping sound of a culture well on its way to spiritual death.

The following is my adaptation of an anonymous piece entitled "The Paradox of Our Time."[6] It summarizes well the spiritual needs of the culture at large.

> The paradox of our time is that we have
> multiplied our possessions, but reduced our values.
> We talk too much, love too seldom, and hate too much.
> We've learned how to make a living, but not a life.
> We've added years to life, not life to years.
>
> These are days of two incomes, but more divorce;
> of fancier houses, but broken homes.
> These are days of throw-away morality, one-night stands,
> overweight bodies, and pills that do everything from cheer,
>   to quiet, to kill.
> It's a time when the lights are on, but no one is at home.

Western societies have become morally and spiritually rudderless. Crime, drug abuse, disintegration of the family, and terrorism are external symptoms of internal deficiencies of our souls. Amidst the loneliness and confusion of Western society many are searching for the "who" and "why" in a world of the "what" and "how."

Soul Care and the Needs of the Church

THE CHURCH IS not free from the spiritual malaise that has so afflicted the culture. Deep spiritual needs are rampant among Christian laity, seminarians, and the clergy as well.

Among Laity

A shocking lack of spiritual discipline exists in the church, reports George Barna. "Four out of ten born again Christians do not attend church or read the Bible in a typical week, three out of ten say they are not 'absolutely committed to the Christian faith,' and seven out of ten are not involved in a small group that meets for spiritual purposes." According to Barna, "There are more than ten million born again Christians who are unchurched."[7]

A shameful ignorance of essential Christian beliefs characterizes the church. Many professing Christians believe that the Holy Spirit is not a person but only a symbol of God's power, Satan does not exist, and that there are many valid paths to heaven. Sadly, people who claim to be born-again are as likely to consult astrological charts and fortune-tellers as are nonChristians.

A Barna study involving 4,000 adults reports that Christian couples have a higher divorce rate than nonChristians. Some 34 percent of nondenominational Christians, 29 percent of Baptist couples, and 21 percent of Catholic couples are divorced. This compares to only 21 percent of atheist or agnostic couples who are divorced. Barna concludes, "The high incidence of divorce within the Christian community challenges the idea that churches provide truly practical and life-changing support for marriages."[8] Is this due in part to the fact that less than one of every five Christian couples pray together?[9]

And in terms of vibrant Christian experience—there is a sad lack here, as well. In a 1998 survey of religious attitudes, Barna discovered that 48 percent of adults who regularly attend Christian churches say they have not experienced God's presence at any time in the past twelve months. Fully 36 percent of born-again Christians indicate that they are still searching for meaning in life.[10]

Many Christians admit they experience God's presence in their lives only sporadically—perhaps at conversion, in a rare mountaintop experience, or during a crisis—rather than day by day. More often, common experience results in laments like these:

> "I've been converted for years. I'm involved in church activities, I know my Bible—and I tithe. But my contact with God is distant, and my sense of communion with Him is nonexistent. Truth be told, I'm dying spiritually and emotionally."

> "I've been a Christian and attended church for many years. But I have no idea what it means to have a relationship with Jesus. God is someone I pray to at night between the sheets when I am in trouble."

> A fifty-something church elder, who has been a Christian for thirty years, relates: "I attend church regularly with my family. But I know more about God with my head than with my heart. I read the Bible perhaps once a month. I pray sporadically— hardly ever with my wife and family. I long to know God personally and to be a more committed Christian. But when I try to go forward with God, I stumble badly."

Three miles from our home, in the opposite direction of Columbine, John Bishop, age 41, lived with his wife, Sherrill, and three beautiful children, ages 6 through 9. Friends and neighbors described the Bishops as a "model family" and the children as "the love of John's life." In addition to being caring parents, John and Sherrill were faithful Sunday school teachers in a flourishing evangelical church. One evening after the family had retired, John removed a small caliber rifle from a closet and shot his sleeping wife, then went into the children's rooms and shot them while they slept. The coroner determined that John was legally drunk at the time of the shootings. A distraught family member said, "It was just despair on John's part."[11]

It seems that churches known for excellent preaching and teaching, "full-service programming," and sending missionaries overseas often fail to minister bedrock soul nourishment to those in the pews—until a life crisis compels intervention. Many churchgoers are crying out silently for help. "Most Christians," Dallas Willard asserts, paraphrasing Thoreau, "live lives of quiet desperation."[12]

Among Seminarians

Many sincere young people preparing for service as pastors and missionaries also struggle in their walks with Christ. From seminaries all around the nation come these reports:

> One student who served as a youth minister for three years says, "I've been in a dry spell in my walk with God, perhaps even in spiritual bankruptcy. I have not been able to forgive myself for the things I have done in the past. Guilt, fear, and holding God at a distance dominate my life."

> Another, with overseas mission experience, laments: "I have neglected the care and nurture of my soul. I'm on a sinking ship. Water is pouring into my vessel."

> A woman who ministered for several years in a Christian campus ministry describes herself as "a success and activity-driven person who has little time for God." She speaks painfully of "the ministry monster that has mastered me."

> Another seminarian admits, "My daily living does not measure up to the level of my knowledge of the faith. I doubt that I'm living the redeemed life to any great extent. My life is no different than that of an unbeliever."

Some future ministers and missionaries enter seminary with poor images of God and self. Others struggle with wounds from dysfunctional family environments. Still others cannot escape secret sins, and live imprisoned in guilt, anxiety, and depression. These idealistic students often represent the best in our churches. They deeply long to succeed in the Christian life, but don't know how to pull it off.

Among Clergy

The pressures of ministry have a way of deflating the sturdiest spirit. A recent survey reveals that 20 percent of pastors in the Lutheran Church–Missouri Synod suffer from advanced-stage burnout. Another 20 percent are stuck in low- to mid-grade burnout. One minister reported, "I would quit tomorrow if it wouldn't screw up my retirement."[13]

Testimonies from clergy in other denominations support such statistics.

The pastor of a large independent church puts it this way: "I have been doing ministry for longer than I can recall on a virtually empty tank, masking my immaturity and/or inferiority by accomplishing great things for the kingdom. I find myself on the west bank of the Jordan, unable to cross over to the Promised Land."

A Presbyterian pastor laments, "In ten years of ministry, spiritual life has slowly been sucked out of me. I have been so busy 'doing ministry' that I've lost intimacy with Christ. Maybe 90 percent of the time I find myself walking in the flesh rather than the Spirit."

After several years of ministry a young pastor found himself completely disoriented. "I have a degree in theology and have read the Bible and prayed regularly. But I've experienced a spirit of confusion and desolation that has eroded my faith in God and the church. Recently I confessed to my senior pastor that I don't believe much of anything anymore. It's devastating to be in the position of trying to help others while unable to help myself."

A woman missionary on furlough relates: "After several years of intense ministry burnout, my soul feels like a spiritual, emotional, and relational wasteland. My sense of God's love has vanished. My condition involves shattered trust in God, apathy in all areas of my life, depression, and a feeling of nothingness. How can I be an effective missionary in such a condition?"

Of all the disheartened clergy I've encountered, no one's experience is sadder to recount than Sam's.

Sam was an effective singles leader in a large southern church, who discipled many young professionals. Through his compassion and ministry skills the singles group grew numerically and spiritually. Sam decided to attend seminary two evenings a week to become better equipped for ministry. A preaching course required students to deliver a sermon to a church congregation. As Sam was halfway through the required sermon, he abruptly stopped and said to the congregation, "Folks, I don't believe a word of what I have said to you today."

As the congregation sat there speechless, he walked off the platform. In short order, he left his wife and two young children and filed for divorce.

What is sad about this experience is that Sam fell into a spiritual black hole . . . with no one there to help him out.

From Here . . . Where Do We Go?

FOR MOST PEOPLE in the broader culture a relationship with Jesus, the friend of sinners, remains an elusive ideal. Even for people in the church, the Good Shepherd is a shadowy stranger. After centuries of a vibrant Christian spirituality that ignited the world, calling millions out of darkness, setting souls free from sin, and giving solid direction to people once lost—how did we get to this point? As Adrian van Kaam puts it: "The art of living in Jesus has been lost by many. We have become less sensitive to the gentle presence of the Holy One in our midst. Fascinated by the lights of this earth, we have become blind to the light that is Jesus."[14]

We've come to this point, it seems, because we have neglected a basic truth about soul care: *Spiritual growth does not happen automatically.*

Jesus Himself likened the life of the soul to a seed bursting open into new life (see Matthew 13). The death and cracking open of the old husk is the conversion, when old ways of thinking, believing, seeing, and doing no longer work and come to an end. But beyond that comes the soul's growth into a new way of thinking, believing, seeing, and doing *everything.*

Beyond conversion, soul care is required. Just as a plant requires regular watering and feeding, so faith must be continually nourished to flourish. If we're not advancing in grace through spiritual discipline, we are regressing into spiritual complacency. In such a condition, God becomes unreal in our experience and we become frustrated and unfulfilled.

This is where spiritual direction comes in. Deep down inside, people hunger for a spiritual friend who will come close and not run away when the going gets dark and tough; for a wise counselor who will confront their harmful, misguided choices; for a strong and faithful soul companion who will help distinguish the voice of God from the voices arising from their own confusion—or from diabolical powers.

The "personal spirituality" we hear promoted is an oxymoron. Every one of us needs the help, support, and counsel of a guide who will point the way to God on the homeward journey.

Where do we begin, if we want the kind of soul care that results in real, healthy, inward growth? How do we form good relationships with people who can become spiritual directors and soul friends? To begin with, we would do well to understand the nature of the journey we are on.

The next chapter will address the dynamics of the spiritual journey itself, with its cautions and possibilities.

TRY IT YOURSELF

1. **Identify your most important spiritual needs.**
   Carve out a quiet space in your life, free from distractions and intrusions. Meditate on a passage of Scripture (such as Psalm 107) that extols the God who meets our spiritual needs. Before God, prayerfully identify the most important longings of your heart. Be especially attentive to needs that you may not have recognized before reading this chapter. Then ask your spouse, or a close friend, to offer perspective on the needs he or she perceives in your life.

2. **Consider this . . . and then ask for God's assistance.**
   How might a godly spiritual friend or counselor bring to bear God's provision for these needs? Prayerfully ask God to lead you to such a person. You may be surprised how mightily God answers this deliberate prayer.

Our Spiritual Journey

ANY JOURNEY WE TAKE IN LIFE CAN BE ENRICHING. EVERY TIME WE travel away from the familiarity of home we become involved in a transformational process. How we're transformed depends on what happens along the way and how we respond to it. Our trip also involves an intended destination—say, the beach or the mountains.

The spiritual life has often been likened to a journey, too. For the Christian, our journey involves the ongoing deepening of a relationship with Jesus. The ultimate destination is to be with Christ forever in the glorious home He is preparing for us in heaven (see John 14:2-3), and this is paralleled in our life here on earth by a growing, deepening intimacy with Christ in spirit (see John 14:20).

Because the purpose of spiritual direction is to strengthen our relationship with Jesus, we need to understand how the process of knowing Christ and incorporating His values and priorities in our life takes place.

The Journey of the Soul

IN OUR PHYSICAL and emotional growth we move through infancy, adolescence, adulthood, middle age, and old age. In spirit, our growth is an increasingly intimate relationship with Christ that is meant to continue until the day when we see Him face to face (see 1 John 3:2). God's aim for His children is that we advance in Christ from being "mere infants" and fleshly (see 1 Corinthian 3:1-3; Ephesians 4:14) to becoming "mature" and spiritual (see 1 Corinthians 2:6,15; Ephesians 4:13). Larry Crabb explains: "Life is a journey toward a land we have not yet seen along a path we sometimes cannot find. It is a journey of the soul toward its destiny and its home."[1]

Reflections on Journeying

YEARS AGO MY wife, Elsie, and I, with our newborn daughter, boarded a single-engine mission plane for the trip from northern Nigeria to our home in the southern part of the country. Only a few wispy clouds graced the sky as we lifted off the runway, but an hour into the flight a low cloud layer formed, covering all the familiar landmarks below. The dirt landing strip that was our destination had no navigation beacon. Our pilot searched for a break in the clouds that would allow us to find a bearing, but he found none. After an anxious time, we peered through a small opening in the clouds and identified a landmark that allowed us to set course for home. Eventually we descended through the cloud layer, and the pilot touched down, dodging the aircraft between a few grazing cattle and a stray elephant.

On our spiritual journey of intimacy with God we need clear landmarks and a reliable guide. Augustine said it well, "Christ as God is the homeland where we are going. Christ as Man is the Way we must travel."[2]

Our spiritual growth in Christ involves growing deeper in our love for God and familiarity with His ways, and also deeper in our love for other human beings. In order to achieve the deepening of both loves, we need the direction of a wise and competent guide, because the path is rarely straight and smooth enough to go it alone. Most often the journey is cratered and twisted by spiritual battles, intellectual challenges, emotional struggles, and perhaps dark depressions. But each small step we take with Jesus reinforces character and brings us closer to our destination (see Hebrews 11:13-16).

Scripture suggests that the process of journeying with Christ unfolds in stages: "Here are the stages in the journey of the Israelites when they came out of Egypt. . . . At the LORD's command Moses recorded the stages in their journey" (Numbers 33:1-2). Likewise, early church leaders understood the Christian spiritual life as one of "progression." Irenaeus (d. 200) wrote, "The Creator is always the same, but those who are created must pass from a beginning and through a middle course, a growth and progression. It is for this increase and progress that God has formed them."[3] The spiritual journey is fluid, involving starts, stops, and digressions. Journeying Christians may cease to grow, regress to earlier stages, and experience more than one stage simultaneously. We want to be clear about one thing as we discuss our journey of spiritual growth: There is only one road to heaven, and that is Jesus Christ (see John 14:6).

Nonetheless, if we want to grow healthy and robust in Christian spirit, the journey we take with Jesus must involve two parts: a redemptive aspect and one that is mission-oriented.[4] The disciple will find it necessary to pursue both a redemptive-level journey of personal growth and also a mission-level journey of Christian service. Some believers launch a mission-level journey without making much, if any, progress on the personal, redemptive level; personal failure and weakness overtake many who have tried only to outwardly serve, and they often become casualties in God's army. Others focus on their personal, redemptive journeys without pursuing the outward, mission journey; they become self-absorbed. A competent spiritual director will help the pilgrim integrate these two aspects of Christian growth into one life.

One of the beauties inherent in our call to follow Christ is that our journey will not be identical to that of another follower. This is why many journey models, or patterns, exist in Christian experience. Each one is a path by which the soul deepens relationship and experiences fruitfulness in Christ's service. The journey models we find in history are built upon various pursuits.

For example, there is the *intellectual* pursuit, which focuses on *knowing the truth*. The journeyer studies the Scriptures in order to understand what God has revealed. Correct ideas held first by the mind are believed then to form the entire person. There is also the *contemplative* pursuit, which focuses on *being present to God with the heart*. Through solitude the journeyer opens herself to God's presence and attends to the voice of the Spirit. There is also the pursuit of *social justice,* a journey that stresses *doing love-filled works*. The disciple enters the public arena, engages the needs of a broken world, and labors for a more just social order.

We find helpful and safe journey patterns both in the Bible and in Christian spiritual writings. I encourage you to explore the various patterns and the pursuits they represent. You may be attracted to one model at a certain time in your life; then as your particular circumstances change, you may be drawn to another model.

Biblical Journey Models

WE HEAR IT said that "life is a journey." Biblical characters who journeyed successfully challenge us to imitate their relationships with God and their fruitfulness in service to Him.

Abraham

Abraham's journey began when God called him to pull up stakes, leave his familiar surroundings in the pagan country of Ur, and travel to a foreign land (see Genesis 12:1-2). Abraham obeyed the Lord, and from his loins came the Jewish nation, and eventually the Messiah himself. On his journey Abraham made altars before which he worshipped the Lord, and became so intimately acquainted with God that he was known as "God's friend" (James 2:23). In a great test of faith, the patriarch was prepared to slay his son Isaac in obedience to a higher call. Abraham stumbled along the way, for twice he deceived by implying that Sarah was his sister, and, impatient with God's timetable, produced a son through the Egyptian maiden Hagar. Yet Abraham is remembered as the spiritual head of believers of all ages (see Galatians 3:7-9; Hebrews 11:12).

David

David was the shepherd, king, poet, and warrior who matured into a man after God's own heart (see Acts 13:22). His intimate personal relationship with God is reflected in the more than seventy stirring psalms he wrote. David became Israel's greatest king, expanding her borders from the Nile to the Tigris–Euphrates valley; and from David's own line came Jesus, the Christ (see Romans 1:3). Yet on his journey David sinned greatly, if not frequently. He disobeyed God by taking a census, practicing polygamy, committing adultery with Bathsheba, and murdering her husband, Uriah. Because David loved God deeply, when he sinned, he quickly repented.

Moses

The most adventurous spiritual journey in history was Israel's Exodus from Egypt and pilgrimage to Canaan. Under the leadership of Moses, Israel left forced labor in Egypt and passed through the parted waters of the Red Sea. At Sinai God gave the fledgling nation the Law, renewed the covenant, and then guided them through numerous trials in the wilderness. Moses passed the torch to Joshua, a new guide for their journey, who led Israel through the Jordan on dry ground into the Promised Land. Gregory of Nyssa (d. 394), in *The Life of Moses*, likened the Christian's journey to the Exodus and wilderness wandering.[5] Israel's crossing of the Red Sea, God's presence with His people in the cloud, and the nation entering the Promised Land all reflect parts of the spiritual journey.

New Testament Figures

In the New Testament, Jesus ministered spiritual guidance to many seekers of spiritual reality: for example, He gave direction to the Samaritan woman who parried with Him at Jacob's well; to the three disciples who ascended the Mount of Transfiguration and then descended to the demon-filled plain; to Cleopas and companion who talked with the Stranger along the road and discovered Him in their home; and to Peter in his painful journey of denial followed by gracious restoration. Jesus devoted much time to ministering spiritual direction to the twelve disciples, who—though well-intentioned—misunderstood His mission, failed to keep watch with Him, and fled from the scene after His death.

Historical Journey Models

CENTURIES OF CHURCH history have given us many helpful models of the spiritual journey. The appendix summarizes three of the most important of these: a model of developing love by Bernard of Clairvaux; a model of developing prayer by Teresa of Avila; and a Puritan model of combating sin found in John Bunyan's *The Pilgrim's Progress*. You will want to read these classic journey models, and consider which ones you relate to most meaningfully.

An Integrated, Contemporary Journey Model

BELOW IS A contemporary journey model that incorporates key insights from Scripture and the wisdom of the church (including the models found in the appendix). This is an integrated model that brings together patterns of knowing, being, and doing in the quest for deeper relationship with Christ. What follows is my adaptation of Janet Hagberg and Robert Guelich's six-stage journey model.[6]

Stage One: The Converted Life
The pilgrim journey begins with joyful discovery of God through conversion and the new birth. Although excited about the new life they have found, converts initially are unsure and unsteady in their faith, much as a newborn fawn falters in its first attempts to stand.

Stage Two: The Discipled Life
Young Christians seek growing understanding of the faith by reading Scripture and developing a theology or worldview; they also seek to practice the basics of Christian living. With their limited understanding, new Christians may become rigid in their convictions and may even absolutize some bright idea (for example, speaking in tongues, or soul-winning, or scriptural knowledge) as the *exclusive* key to growth. They may see themselves as the sole purveyors of "the" truth, with others mistaken in their beliefs.

Stage Three: The Productive Life
This is the doing, or the "roll-up-your-sleeves-and-get-busy," stage. Disciples receive the false message that busyness and accomplishments endear them to God. Here Christians may fall into the trap of serving "in the flesh" or seeking the applause of others to boost the ego. They may find themselves pressured into assuming responsibilities before being spiritually prepared. Viewing ministry as performance, servants may lose personal contact with God. A disturbing distance between the soul and God develops, ironically, at the same time disciples appear to be so productive in the "Lord's service." Overextended, they may become embittered and angry with colleagues or with God Himself.

Often in this third stage believers may experience a major crisis—a wrenching, face-to-face encounter with their own inadequacy. The crisis may be precipitated by a natural development (such as a midlife transition), an external event (loss of a job), or a personal condition (a serious illness). Some who once were riding high now feel disillusioned, betrayed, and angry. Some, like Demas (see 2 Timothy 4:10), throw in the towel. But those who genuinely reexamine their relationships with God use the crisis to catch the vision of a new beginning.

Stage Four: The Inward Journey

"Hitting the wall" in stage three serves as the catalyst for pursuing a transforming inner journey. Persuaded that the old pattern does not work, believers enter deeply with the soul to engage God. They may practice spiritual disciplines that foster reflection and prayer; they may take retreats, work with spiritual directors, and experience fresh integration of faith to life. Surprisingly, these people discover that God has been waiting for them all along. The healing of Peter's brokenness (see John 21:15-23) illustrates the transformational nature of this inward journey.

Hagberg and Guelich offer a bold observation: "It would be great to think that most priests, ministers, and other spiritual leaders could be our guide through stage four and the Wall. The sad truth is that many of these leaders have not been led through this stage themselves and have not allowed themselves to question deeply or to become whole. So many of those to whom we look most naturally for help are inadequate guides for this part of the journey."[7] Spiritual directors who have traveled the path offer struggling pilgrims the best hope.

Stage Five: The Outward Journey

God directs those who have made the renewing inward journey back outward into the active world with clear vision and purpose. The call may be to the same ministry, but the motivation is radically different. Filled with deep love for God, disciples now serve not themselves, but the interests of others. Christians who navigate this passage marvel that earlier they were blind to what following Jesus is all about. But in the "productive" stage, "We were just too busy, too noisy, or too successful to see it."[8] Paul's service as Christ's bond slave to the Gentile world illustrates the outward journey stage.

Stage Six: The Journey of Love

Here, the Christian senses God's call to lay down his life in Christ's name for others. Filled with the Father's love, like Jesus, he washes others' feet, either figuratively or literally. "We have little ambition to be well known, rich, successful, noteworthy, goal-oriented, or 'spiritual.' We are like vessels into which

God pours His spirit, constantly overflowing."[9] In this stage servants live simply and sacrificially because their focus is God and His priorities. Disregarding success and reputation, they appear to others to have wasted their lives. The elderly apostle John illustrates well the life of selfless love (see 1 John).

This model challenges all of us as disciples to pursue the crucial inner journey. It issues a call to move from being superficial and circumferential people to being inner-directed, God-centered people. As Thomas à Kempis put it, "The inward person [God] visits often and brings pleasant conversation, much peace, and friendship better than your highest expectation."[10]

A respected pastor, who understood this journey pattern, shares this: "I have lived in the productive stage for most of my ministry. But by reading the spiritual classics and learning about the conscious inner journey my life and ministry have been revolutionized." An experienced missionary who met this model in a class wept as we discussed the performance stage of the journey. She confessed, "For years I have been performing for God rather than serving Him out of love."

This journey model helps us understand why successful journeyers are sometimes misunderstood. Reflecting the stages of spiritual growth, psychiatrist and author M. Scott Peck notes that people are attracted to Christians who are one journey stage ahead of them. But often they are cowed by folks who are two stages ahead of them, because they lack personal experience of the more advanced stages. Peck writes, "If people are one step ahead of us we usually admire them. If they are two steps ahead of us, we usually think they are evil. That's why Socrates and Jesus were killed; they were thought to be evil."[11]

The biblical and historical journey models provide a framework for the spiritual needs that exist in the culture and church, as discussed in chapter 2. The models also highlight the challenges and rewards on the journey of deepening relationship with Christ. Believers advance by joining hands with a spiritual friend or guide who will present a clearer vision of the treasures God has in store for them (see 1 Corinthians 2:9).

TRY IT YOURSELF

1. Reflect on your personal spiritual journey.

Which of the journey models speak most directly to your life experience? Why?

Where are you currently on the spiritual journey?

Are you satisfied with your progress on the pilgrim path? Can you identify those factors that might be hindering your spiritual progress?

2. Have you experienced a life crisis – physical, emotional, vocational, or spiritual – that beckons you to deeper relationship with the Lord?

The Father often uses difficulties to deepen relationship with Jesus. How did you respond to its pressures and with what outcomes?

Walter Brueggemann observes, "Our life of faith consists in moving with God through a recurring pattern of (a) being securely *oriented*, (b) being painfully *disoriented*; and (c) being surprisingly *reoriented*."

Being securely *oriented* "is a situation of equilibrium. While we all yearn for it, it is not very interesting and it does not produce great prayer or powerful song." This is "the mood of much of the middle-class church."[12] Being painfully *disoriented* is an experience of dislocation that overcomes inertia and urges us to open up to God. Old Testament psalms of lament or complaint (see Psalms 13, 44, 80) rehearse the experience of disorientation and distress. Being surprisingly *reoriented* refers to the experience of being made new by touching the heart of God. Psalms of praise (see Psalms 103, 116, 138, 145) celebrate this liberating experience.

Discuss with a friend or spouse this suggestive journey pattern of being oriented, disoriented, and reoriented.

Have you passed through an experience that could be called disorienting? If so, describe its effects.

How might such an experience have reoriented you to significant spiritual growth?

Did God use any human spiritual guides in this process?

Discipleship, Mentoring, and Spiritual Direction

WHETHER TAKING A FLOAT TRIP DOWN A RIVER OR SCALING A HIGH mountain, we profit from having a reliable guide. When it comes to the spiritual journey, it's helpful to understand the various guides there are to help and accompany us on our way.

In particular, it's important to recognize the distinctions between several different types of "helping" ministries — namely, discipleship, mentoring, spiritual direction, and counseling. While these ministries are somewhat flexible, each has a specific focus and goal. Because we need guides to help us on our way, and not every one is the same, it's important to understand the distinctive features of each type of guidance, and the relationship between them, as well.

Evangelism

THE TV PROGRAM *Dateline NBC* followed Boston oncologist Dr. Jerome Groopman for two years as he worked to save patients Gene Brown (suffering from AIDS) and Elizabeth Sanderson (suffering from breast cancer). Through the treatment process the doctor came to know his patients intimately. He watched both come to grips with their illnesses, and saw Sanderson come to faith in Christ. Both eventually succumbed to their diseases. From this ordeal Dr. Groopman concluded, "If you care for someone without addressing his or her soul, you're not really caring for them."[1]

The starting point for the journey of growth must be evangelism — the ministry that introduces a preChristian to Jesus Christ and launches the new convert on the lifelong spiritual journey. Evangelism focuses on issues of sin, conversion, and trust in Christ as Savior and Lord. Every Christian-helping ministry builds on this foundation.

The essential message of evangelism is, "Here is what you must do in order to become a child of God." But then the question arises: After evangelism . . . what next?

Spiritual Formation

SADLY, THE CHURCH has often been unclear, or shortsighted, as to what must take place in the life of the new believer *after* conversion. Let me state it in the simplest way: After conversion we will spend the rest of our lives engaged in the process of spiritual formation. For many, this is a new or vague term.

Spiritual formation concerns the shaping of our life after the pattern of Jesus Christ. It's a process that takes place in the inner person, whereby our character is reshaped by the Spirit. This doesn't mean that it's an entirely private, personal matter. Rather, it's meant to result in a new kind of outward activity, motivated by the new character of Christ in us, both in the body of Christ (the church) and in the world, as we live out the Savior's values in service to others. In the words of Christian philosopher Dallas Willard, "Spiritual formation in the Christian tradition is a process of increasingly being possessed and permeated by the fruit of the Spirit as we walk in the easy yoke of discipleship with Jesus as our teacher."[2] Many Scriptures describe this lifelong process of spiritual formation, including 2 Corinthians 3:18, Galatians 4:19, Ephesians 4:13,22-24, Colossians 3:9-10, and 1 Thessalonians 5:23.

Discipleship

FOR SOME CHRISTIANS, spiritual formation is a new and somewhat foreign term, though it's much older than another one with which we're more familiar — discipleship.

Discipleship is the ministry that seeks to teach new believers essential Christian beliefs, and also to train us in practices that are normal in the unfolding spiritual journey. Many of these practices are new to us, and require training.

The essential message of discipleship is, "Here is what you need to know, do, or become."[3]

Discipleship often occurs in structured programs of limited duration, and it's assumed that we are "discipled" when we've completed a ten- or twelve-week program. Discipleship deals with the basics of Christian belief: Bible study methods, cultivating a devotional life, sharing one's faith, discovery of spiritual gifts, and stewardship of resources. Discipleship ministries provide young Christians with the "milk" or "elementary truths of God's word" (Hebrews 5:12). They are a necessary foundation for the maturing of pilgrims on the spiritual journey.

A gifted campus minister writes, "The discipleship program I know was a structured, short-term program that trained converts in the basics of Christian living. It succeeded in equipping trainees in the essentials of the faith, but took them only so far. It fell short of preparing them for the inevitable questions and crises they would face later in their journeys." The ministry of spiritual direction, she later discovered, took up where the short-term discipleship program left off.

Richard V. Peace, of Fuller Seminary, tells of being discipled by a program that includes church attendance, Bible reading, believing the right things, prayer, and witnessing. "We did pretty well at the *knowing,* okay at the *doing,* but the whole question of *being* was fraught with difficulty. The real issue was internal. Something else was needed."[4] Peace concludes that in order to *become,* true disciples of Jesus will benefit greatly by supplementing helpful, short-term discipleship programs with lifelong patterns of spiritual formation and direction. We can also benefit by reading neglected spiritual classics, and by practicing a range of spiritual disciplines, taking retreats, and tempering our action-oriented Western lifestyle with the balance of a more contemplative pace.

Mentoring

MENTORING IS THE process whereby someone who is more experienced at a given skill teaches, models, and imparts essential knowledge, skills, and strategies to someone less experienced. The Uncommon Individual Foundation describes the essence of mentoring: "an older person providing knowledge and advice on a one-to-one basis to a younger, less experienced person, the mentoree."[5]

The spirit of the mentoring relationship is that the mentor imparts these things freely, in order to help the protégés attain goals that are their own. It is not mentoring, but something else, if we try to recreate people in our own image, or to accomplish goals that are ours, not theirs. Gordon Shea describes a mentor as one of those special people in life who, through his deeds and words, helps another person move toward the fulfillment of his individual potential.

The essential message of mentoring ministry is, "How can I help you get where you are going?"[6]

Through teaching, modeling, and coaching, mentoring is primarily a task-oriented service. Fred Smith observes, "Mentoring is a one-on-one relationship between a mentor and a mentoree for the specific and definable development of a skill or an art."[7] Mentoring first took root in the fields of industry and education before being adopted by the church. It is not improper to speak of spiritual mentoring, but there is some truth in the statement that the mentoring model's "association with academia makes it less than ideal in the pastoral context."[8]

A disciplined Christian businessman mentors a young couple struggling to get out of debt and manage their finances. A pastor with twenty years experience mentors a young seminary graduate who wishes to develop a singles' ministry. One mentoring article in a Christian magazine encourages protégés to select a mentor who is more experienced, has a track record of success, possesses greater spiritual depth, and who earns more money.[9] Most who understand the goals of spiritual mentoring would accept all but that last criterion.

Spiritual Guidance

TO THIS POINT, I've been using the specific term *spiritual direction*. Here, I would like to broaden my reference in order to look at a range of important soul-care ministries that fall under the umbrella of spiritual guidance. At a minimum, these include spiritual friendship, spiritual counsel, as well as spiritual direction.

Spiritual guidance refers to any help given individually or in a group that advances the process of spiritual formation. *Guide* is a biblical term meaning "one who shows the way" (see Romans 2:19). The word *guide* *(hodegos)* is the root of the related biblical term *guardian* or *trainer* *(paidagogas,* see 1 Corinthians 4:15). Spiritual guidance is the helping ministry that forms Christlikeness in us as we move through life on our journey of discipleship. While it is important to understand that God is the principal guide of us, His people (Psalm 48:14), He nonetheless graciously provides human guides to lead us into His most holy presence.

The essential message of spiritual guidance is, "Together, we're going to pay prayerful attention to God's gracious working in your life."

If discipleship focuses on the disciple and mentoring on the protégé, spiritual guidance focuses uniquely on the individual's growing relationship with God. Spiritual guidance works in the field of sacred space, which is to say, in the soul. Its prayerful, contemplative approach gives it a distinctively transcendent orientation. And its goal is to clear the inner ground of the soul so that more of the character of God, more of the actions willed by God for this particular life, can be manifested through the individual Christian.

It may be helpful to take a clear look at some of the distinctions that exist between the ministries I've grouped here under the heading of spiritual guidance.

SPIRITUAL FRIENDSHIP	SPIRITUAL COUNSEL	SPIRITUAL DIRECTION
Informal, Unstructured, Reciprocal		Formal, Structured, One-Directional
Long-term	Occasional	Intensive

Spiritual Friendship

Spiritual friendship is the most basic ministry of spiritual guidance in which two or more friends—on a relatively equal basis—support, encourage, and pray for one another on their journeys. This informal ministry reflects the centuries-old "soul friend" tradition in Christianity. In Latin, the word *friend (amicus)* comes from the word for "love" *(amor)*. Thus, friends are persons who join hands in a covenant of love. Some of the most fruitful occasions of spiritual guidance occur in serendipitous moments between friends who open their hearts to each other and share their dreams. A spiritual friend is one who makes time for you, cares when you have nothing to offer in return, rejoices over your successes, and weeps over your failures. Aelred of Rievaulx (d. 1167) noted that Christ kisses us through the love of our friends.

In Scripture, David and Jonathan made a covenant of friendship before the Lord—even though Jonathan's father, Saul, was insanely jealous of David. Solomon wrote, "Friends love through all kinds of weather" (Proverbs 17:17, MSG). Jesus and the disciples were soul friends (see John 15:15), as were He and Mary, Martha and Lazarus (see John 11:11). Today, when two or three men help one another by offering spiritual counsel to get through life's confusing maze, or when they work together building a home with Habitat for Humanity, they are in both cases practicing spiritual friendship.

Spiritual Counsel

Spiritual counsel refers to the occasional helping ministry in which a godly Christian offers focused help to another person who seeks to know God and His will. One may offer spiritual counsel through a personal conversation, letter, or sermon. The elderly priest Eli offered spiritual counsel to young Samuel who sought to discern God's call upon his life (see 1 Samuel 3:1-9). Solomon wrote, "The heartfelt counsel of a friend is as sweet as perfume and incense" (Proverbs 27:9, NLT). Paul's letter to Philemon concerning his runaway slave, Onesimus, is an excellent biblical example of spiritual counsel. Today, a mature woman who offers a word of biblical wisdom to a young wife who is suffering from a life-draining sense of spiritual dryness ministers spiritual counsel.

Spiritual Direction

Spiritual direction was defined in chapter one as "the ministry of soul care in which a gifted and experienced Christian helps another person to grow in relationship with and obedience to God by following the example of Jesus Christ." According to Henri Nouwen, "A spiritual director is not a counselor, a therapist, or an analyst, but a mature fellow Christian to whom we choose to be accountable for our spiritual life and from whom we can expect prayerful guidance in our constant struggle to discern God's active presence in our lives."[10] Spiritual direction is an important form of pastoral care.

Spiritual direction has a long and distinguished history in the church. After years of neglect, we are revisiting this time-honored ministry because we all need support in order to grow up in Christ. Some Protestants may find the term *spiritual direction* unsettling because of its potential for authoritarianism and for minimizing the priesthood of every believer. But as Larry Crabb notes, "No other term seems to carry less baggage." The terms *mentor* and *disciple* "have mechanistic overtones that miss the fluid dynamic of the Spirit's sovereign movement."[11]

God the Holy Spirit is, of course, the true spiritual director who relentlessly pursues Christlikeness in His children. But the human director, as the Spirit's instrument, is a midwife who brings forth new spiritual life; a careful "plowman" who redirects the other from the surface events of life to the spiritual understrata in order to cultivate the soul's "soil" for growth; and a codiscerner who catches the gentle breezes of the Holy Spirit.

Spiritual direction is a highly personalized ministry, respecting individual life histories, temperaments, levels of maturity, and vocations. G. Campbell Morgan offered this observation: "Let those who have the cure of souls in any form not stereotype their methods. If you have somewhere a book giving mechanical instructions as to how to deal with souls, go straight home and burn it! Why? Because the next soul you meet will baffle your textbooks and laugh at your regulations. Humanity is infinite in variety."[12]

The goals of spiritual direction are threefold. In the area of knowing, the spiritual director helps the directee understand God's will as revealed in Scripture and illumined by faithful spiritual writings. In the realm of being, the director prays for the transformation of the directee's inner world after the image of Christ. In the realm of doing, the director encourages the directee to faithfully live out the gospel in the power of the Spirit.

When Tammy graduated from seminary she received no offers for a position in youth ministry. She began to doubt God's call upon her life. Had she made a poor choice by going to seminary? Anxiously, the young woman asked herself and a few close friends, "What does God want me to do?" An older Christian, gifted in spiritual direction, gently responded, "Tammy, I believe you're asking the wrong question. You should be asking, 'What does God want me to *be?*'" The wise elder knew that God is first interested in who we *are,* and then interested in what we *do.*

The spiritual director helps the one seeking direction to process her relationship with God, uncovers resistances to growth, lays bare hidden pockets of sin, guides the practice of spiritual disciplines, facilitates listening to God, and encourages the life of prayer. In short, he or she clears the interior ground of the soul and replants in it the living Word of God in order to nurture the release of the life of Christ from within. The spiritual director will listen, question, rephrase, suggest, offer responses, and pray with and for the one seeking direction—while resisting the temptation to be merely an advice giver or problem solver.

In Scripture, Naomi guided Ruth, her Moabitess daughter-in-law, to faith in Yahweh and later to marriage with the godly kinsman Boaz. Nathan ministered spiritual direction to David when he helped bring to light pockets of darkness in the king's heart and his sins of adultery and murder. We will explore Jesus' many spiritual-direction encounters in part 2 of this book. Paul's letters to Timothy and Titus offer individual spiritual direction, whereas many of his letters to local churches are powerful letters of direction for the common good.

Counseling

PSYCHOLOGICAL COUNSELING IS the ministry that seeks personality growth, resolution of inner conflicts, and more efficient interpersonal functioning. This kind of counseling is initiated by an anxiety-laden problem or crisis, advances through personal discovery and growth, and ends with the resolution of the presenting problem. An important healing factor is the client-counselor relationship.

The essential message of counseling therapy is, "How can I help resolve your problem or relieve your pain?"

God created us as whole beings, in such a way that body, mind, emotions, and soul all interconnect. Our physical health and emotional states invariably affect our spiritual life. Conversely, our spiritual state affects our physical and emotional well-being. For this reason I believe it's virtually impossible to separate out our emotional from our spiritual issues. Many Christians testify that as they deepen relationships with Christ, their emotional health improves. It's also my belief that if the redemptive ministry of spiritual guidance were more widely practiced by God's people, the need for psychological counseling would be reduced.

Pastoral counseling is a related short-term ministry that involves helping persons manage life's pressures and problems. It may address a problem that needs fixing, a relationship that needs mending, or a decision that needs to be made. Pastoral counseling occurs within a theological framework and draws upon biblical wisdom and resources. Many pastoral counselors are rediscovering the life-giving resources of spiritual direction for themselves, and also learning how to offer spiritual direction to those under their care.

Relating the Soul-Care Ministries

HOW DO THE ministries of discipleship, mentoring, spiritual guidance, and counseling relate to one another? Although they are different ministries, in practice they interact. A Christian care-giver may, in fact, find himself called upon to be involved in each of the ministries briefly outlined above. For example, someone involved in discipling may find it necessary to mentor someone to help that person learn a ministry task. A spiritual director may help someone navigate a midlife transition. Or a Christian therapist may nourish a client's prayer life.

It may be helpful to think of the four ministries by comparing them to specializations in medicine. In dealing with patients, an internist, for example, may address a medical problem in the area of cardiology. Given his or her training and experience, a pastor may be called upon to minister discipleship, mentoring, spiritual guidance, and pastoral counseling, in much the same way that a general-practice physician is called upon to deal with a wide variety of medical issues. And just as a patient may need more than one medical specialist to resolve a health problem, so a growing Christian may need to consult more than one spiritual care-giver to facilitate growth in both wholeness and holiness.

And so, the distinctive but interactive nature of the four ministries can be represented as four sides of a pyramid, held together by the overarching purpose (or point) of biblical discipleship. For in the end, we are to love God with the strength and energy of our whole being, living out the comprehensive discipleship commanded by Jesus Himself.

Biblical Discipleship (Matthew 28:19)

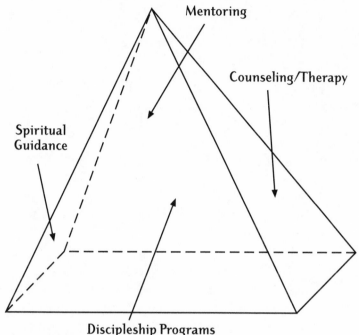

Mentoring

Counseling/Therapy

Spiritual
Guidance

Discipleship Programs

TRY IT YOURSELF

1. Revisiting Your Personal Questions and Struggles

Recall from the previous chapter the stages of the spiritual journey. Where on this journey have you experienced spiritual or emotional struggles?

What "crisis" might God have used to cause reevaluation and stimulate growth in your life?

Share your perspectives with a trusted and sensitive spiritual friend.

2. Assessing Christian Helping Ministries

On your journey thus far, which of the helping ministries discussed has stimulated your spiritual growth the most?

From reading this chapter, have you been challenged to seek out other helping ministries?

Which ministry holds a special attraction for you?

Soul Care Through the Centuries

IN THE PREVIOUS CHAPTER WE LOOKED AT THE VARIOUS MINISTRIES involved in spiritual guidance to see how they all relate to the more specific ministry of spiritual direction. In this chapter we want to look briefly at spiritual guidance as it's been practiced in the church through the centuries. This can help us to better understand in our own time how to offer this ministry and how to personally benefit from it.

The Early Church

DURING THE DECLINE of the Roman Empire in the third and fourth centuries, some twenty thousand Christians fled for refuge into the deserts of Palestine, Syria, Egypt, and Arabia. Many believed they were following the path of Elijah, John the Baptist, and Jesus, each of whom withdrew to the wilderness to meet God (see Hebrew 11:38). The desert Christians sought out godly "fathers" *(abbas)* and "mothers" *(ammas)* who, in the harsh desert environment, urged purity of heart, pointed out obstacles to spiritual growth, and helped in the discernment of spirits. Antony of Egypt (d. 356), Evagrius Ponticus (d. 399), and John Cassian (d. 435) were leading desert fathers. The spiritual counsel of the *abbas* and *ammas* was offered one-on-one, in small gatherings, and later in monastic communities.

Here is a sampling of the wisdom preserved in *The Sayings of the Desert Fathers*:

> Abba Pambo came to Abba Antony and said, "Give me a word father," and he said: "Do not trust in your own righteousness; do not grieve about a sin that is past and gone; and keep your tongue and your belly under control."[1]

> Abba Joseph said to Abba Nisterus, "What should I do about my tongue, for I cannot control it?" The old man said to him, "When you speak, do you find peace?" He replied, "No." The old man said, "If you do not find peace, why do you speak? Be silent and when a conversation takes place, it is better to listen than to speak."[2]

Basil (d. 379), bishop of Caesarea, urged Christians to find a suitable person "who may serve you as a very sure guide in the work of leading a holy life," one who knows "the straight road to God." Basil warned, "To believe that one does not need counsel is great pride."[3] Ambrose of Milan (d. 397), theologian and preacher, offered Christ-centered spiritual guidance to new Christians through personal conversation, letters, and treatises. Augustine (d. 430), the brilliant churchman and theologian, ministered spiritual guidance through personal conversations and letters of spiritual counsel.

Spiritual direction took on an institutional flavor in monastic communities throughout the Christian world. The abbot, or spiritual father, guided the community in the ascetic life according to each person's needs. Benedict (d. 547), author of the famous *Rule*, offered guidelines for the spiritual formation of the community that remain in use today.

Celtic Christianity in Ireland and Britain flourished from the fifth century onward and focused on the ministry of the soul friend, or *anamcara*. From this tradition, represented by Patrick (d. 460) and Columba (d. 597), founder of the community at Iona, came the saying, "Anyone without a soul friend is a body without a head."[4]

The Middle Ages

GREGORY THE GREAT (d. 604), who stressed the importance of Scripture and the monastic way of life, was a renowned master of spiritual formation. Gregory's famous *Pastoral Rule* offers profound insights into the ministry of soul care. For Gregory, "The art of ruling souls is the art of arts."[5]

Centuries later, Bernard of Clairvaux (d. 1153), the Cistercian abbot, preacher, and writer, penned more than 460 letters of spiritual counsel that encouraged, exhorted, and rebuked seekers. Bernard wrote, "He who sets himself up as his own teacher becomes the pupil of a fool."[6]

Aelred of Rievaulx (d. 1167), the famous author of *Spiritual Friendship*, was widely consulted on matters of spiritual guidance. Aelred was a servant and friend to seekers, rather than their superior. According to Aelred, "The gospel life, with all its twists and turns, is too much for us to handle alone. We need the counsel, guidance, and support of others who will tread the path with us. That person is the spiritual friend." He added, "To live without friends is to live like a beast."[7]

In his classic work, *The Imitation of Christ*, Thomas à Kempis (d. 1471) urged Christians who sought to know Christ more fully to "ask counsel from a person of sound judgment; ask instruction from one better than you; avoid following your own proud ideas."[8]

Reformation Onward

AVOIDING AUTHORITARIANISM AND emphasizing the priesthood of the individual believer, the Protestant Reformers also understood the need for soul care. In his influential *Letters of Spiritual Counsel*, Martin Luther (d. 1546) offered spiritual guidance to searching souls from many walks of life. John Calvin (d. 1564) was as much a pastor and guide of souls as a theologian and scholar. He too wrote many letters of spiritual guidance, such that posterity has assigned him the title, "Director of Souls." The French Reformer Martin Bucer (d. 1551) contributed to spiritual guidance as well, in his work *On the True Cure of Souls*.

Ignatius of Loyola (d. 1556) made a major contribution to soul care through his famous *Spiritual Exercises*, a manual for spiritual directors leading guided retreats. The *Exercises* focuses on several foundational subjects, including the discernment of good and evil spirits, deepening of prayer, and identifying God's will. Ignatius insisted that the person without a soul friend is like a body without a head.

Teresa of Avila (d. 1582), the Carmelite Reformer, saw formal spiritual direction as the key to renewal of the church. She claimed that a journeyer needs a learned and experienced spiritual director to make progress. Reflecting on her personal experience, Teresa wrote, "Self-reliance was what destroyed me. For this reason and for every reason there is need of a master and for discussions with spiritual persons."[9] She added, "Every Christian should try to consult some learned person if he can, and the more learned the person the better. Those who walk in the way of prayer have the greater need of learning; and the more spiritual they are, the greater is their need."[10]

John of the Cross (d. 1591), the famous compatriot of Teresa, insisted that while God Himself is the Lord and Guide of every life, nonetheless the soul needs spiritual guides that act as the gentle instruments of the Spirit to lead us in our transformation in Christ. Many Christians make little progress, John said, "because they understand not themselves and lack competent and alert directors who will guide them to the summit."[11]

Frances of Sales (d. 1622), Bishop of Geneva, guided souls with counsel and advice, not commands. Concerning the spiritual director, he wrote, "Find someone to guide you. It is . . . the surest way to find the will of God. . . . When you have found him, look on him as an angel, not merely a man."[12]

The seventeenth- and eighteenth-century Puritan preachers were skilled physicians of the soul. Their spiritual guidance focused on life struggles, temptations, and discernment of spiritual states. Puritan guides watched over souls by asking questions such as, "How effective is your prayer life?" "Are you growing in Christ?" and "Are you actively resisting the Devil?" Puritan pastors also gave guidance through correspondence and in treatises dealing with practical spiritual matters. Some of the best-known examples include *Discouragement's Recovery,* by Richard Sibbes (d. 1635), and *A Child of Light Walking in Darkness,* by Thomas Goodwin (d. 1680).

The Church of England has highly valued spiritual direction since its inception. Bishop and theologian Jeremy Taylor (d. 1667) wrote, "God hath appointed spiritual persons as guides for souls, whose office it is to direct and to comfort, to give peace and to conduct, to refresh the weary and to strengthen the weak; and therefore to use their advice is that proper remedy which God hath appointed."[13] Preaching alone, he insisted, is inadequate to address the complex needs of believers on their homeward journeys.

In his book *The Reformed Pastor,* Richard Baxter (d. 1691) cited four classes of people in need of spiritual counsel: those who are Christian in name only (the unconverted), those who are young and weak in the faith, Christians fallen into sin who need to be restored, and the strong. He believed the last group needs the greatest attention.[14]

François Fénelon (d. 1715), bishop, preacher, and spiritual director, offered counsel to Christians serious about spiritual growth in both one-on-one conferences and through correspondence. Topics of his letters include, "How to Talk With God," "Dryness and Deadness in Prayer," and "When Feelings Fail Us."[15]

Although the Society of Friends (Quakers) stressed the doctrine of the "inner light," by which God speaks directly to the soul, George Fox (d. 1691) wrote more than three thousand letters that directed seekers to experiential knowledge of Christ, holiness of life, and practical Christian living. The journals of Fox and John Woolman (d. 1772) also served as helpful vehicles of spiritual guidance.

John Wesley (d. 1791) very clearly ministered spiritual guidance through the network of Methodist class meetings across Britain, devoted to growth in holiness. These groups of a dozen persons plus a leader met for purposes of mutual spiritual nurture that included confession, encouragement, and challenge.

Modern Times

LEST WE CONTEMPORARY Christians think that the ministry of spiritual direction "trailed off" before modern times began, this important work has in fact continued into our day.

Evelyn Underhill (d. 1941), an Anglican authority on mysticism, claimed that each Christian needs a competent colistener, discerner, and resource person for the journey. Reginald Somerset Ward (d. 1962) wrote, "The task of the spiritual director . . . is not that he should be a judge or a dictator issuing commands, but that he should be a physician of souls whose main work is to diagnose the ills of the soul and the hindrances to its contact with God; and to find, as far as he is given grace, a cure for them."[16]

C. S. Lewis (d. 1963), the beloved author and Oxford don, served as a spiritual guide in three areas. First, as a scholar for thirty years at Oxford University, he showed deep concern for the spiritual needs of students. Second, he preached in churches, colleges, and on BBC Radio during the dark days of World War II, offering soul guidance to an entire nation. Finally, in his extensive correspondence with acquaintances and strangers, he helped countless men, women, and young people who were seeking spiritual support. One noteworthy example is Lewis' *Letters to an American Lady*, written to a Roman Catholic widow on a wide range of subjects. For Lewis, spiritual direction asks, (1) "What is God's joy for me?" (2) "What is my present duty?" and (3) "What is real?"[17]

Thomas Merton (d. 1968), the Trappist monk who converted to Christ while a student at Columbia University, also exercised his gift of spiritual direction through personal conversations, extensive correspondence, and many popular writings. For Merton, "a spiritual director is one who helps another to recognize and to follow the inspirations of grace in his life, in order to arrive at the end to which God is leading him."[18]

Taking Stock

Dallas Willard summarizes the history of soul care in the church this way: "Spiritual direction was understood by Jesus, taught by Paul, obeyed by the early church, followed with excesses in the medieval church, narrowed by the Reformers, recaptured by the Puritans, and virtually lost in the modern church."

As we've seen, spiritual direction has been an important formational ministry in the Christian church since the outset. As Eugene Peterson puts it, "For most of the history of the Christian faith it was expected that a person would have a spiritual director."[19] But life-giving spiritual direction has been much neglected in the modern church. Peterson adds, "There is nothing in our culture, and very little even in our churches, that encourages the work of spiritual direction."[20]

A personal friend, a pastor, echoes Peterson's sentiment: "As I look back on my spiritual journey, I cannot specifically recall any real spiritual guides,

mentors, or directors in my life. I feel so lacking in this area of ministry."
Given the centrality of this important ministry, why have we in today's
church experienced so little in the way of spiritual direction? There are
many reasons for this lack.

Primarily, Western culture stresses individual self-reliance.
Unfortunately, this thinking permeates the church today, as well. Also, our
culture worships the god of productivity rather than cherishing interpersonal relationships. Often in the church, our emphasis is on such measur-
able, productive activities as "soul winning" or "program building." The
current neglect of spiritual direction may also be due to Hellenistic thinking that views life in linear, mechanistic fashion. We tend to believe that the
spirit grows in the same way as the mind thinks: A + B + C = D. If you
want to get to your goal (D), then you must go through certain logical steps
(A, B, and C). Such reasoning, of course, leaves little room for God's work
in our lives, which oftentimes defies straightforward logic.

Henri Nouwen lamented the neglect of spiritual direction in our day:

> Many ministers today are excellent preachers, competent coun-
> selors, and good program administrators, but few feel comfort-
> able giving spiritual direction to people who are searching for
> God's presence in their lives. For many ministers, if not for
> most, the life of the Holy Spirit is unknown territory. It is not
> surprising, therefore, that many unholy spirits have taken over
> and created considerable havoc. There is an increasing need for
> diagnosticians of the soul who can distinguish the Holy Spirit
> from the unholy spirits and so guide people to an active and
> vital transformation of soul and body, and of all their personal
> relationships.[21]

A recent issue of *Leadership* magazine describes how five experienced
pastors were forced to reassess their ministries. One pastor said, "I am convicted that I have not been living, functioning, or walking as a shepherd."
Another who resigned from a large congregation wrote, "I quit because I
was miserable . . . I spent most of my time keeping the wheels of the organization greased." A third confessed, "The way I had been doing ministry
was inadequate . . . I suffered from the 'busies.' I was so mired in the minu-
tiae of ministry that I couldn't get above it to provide visionary leadership
. . . I needed to become a spiritual director." He added, "My move to spiritual director has elevated what I do as pastor . . . And in a world with
growing spiritual hunger, [spiritual work] is our best opportunity to guide
people to life-changing faith."[22]

A Grace Reinstated

THIS CHAPTER HAS presented an historical case for the life-giving ministry of spiritual guidance. I agree with Thomas Oden, who said, "The arts of spiritual direction that have been developed, nurtured, reexamined, and refined over a dozen centuries of pastoral experience may be due for serious restudy."[23] In the providence of God such a change is taking place, and an important vehicle of God's grace is being reinstated throughout the whole body of Christ.

Now that we've examined the ministry of spiritual direction and its importance historically in the life of the church, it's time to taste for ourselves what this ministry can mean to us personally. To that end, we'll now explore a broad sampling of Jesus' ministry of spiritual direction as He offered it to men and women of His day who were each struggling through life on individual paths to God. For this sampling, of course, we'll examine encounters Jesus had with a variety of people, with wide-ranging needs and questions, as recorded in the Gospels.

In the end, Jesus is the One we must turn to as our ultimate model, the quintessential spiritual director who can inspire us today as we seek to be, and to guide, His twenty-first-century disciples.

TRY IT YOURSELF

1. **I highly recommend you read a book of wise spiritual counsel.**
   You might choose from among the following:
   Teresa of Avila, *The Way of Perfection* (Paraclete Press, 2000).
   François Fénelon, *Talking with God* (Paraclete Press, 1997).
   C. S. Lewis, *Letters to an American Lady* (Eerdmans, 1967).

2. **Begin to keep a spiritual journal, so you can develop "continuity" in your spiritual life. A journal can help you detect ruts in which you're stuck, as well as important insights you need to apply.**
   Record in your journal several insights from the reading that caused you to say, "Aha!"—that suggest to you potential for spiritual growth. Apply these insights to the desires and needs of your life.

   How do you plan to implement these insights into your personal spiritual journey?

3. **Read a spiritual biography.**
   Read the life of a deeply spiritual person, such as A. W. Tozer or Henri Nouwen, and as you read, pay special attention to the ways this person received important spiritual guidance.

PART 2

JESUS MINISTERING SOUL CARE

Impatient with God's Timing

A N EXECUTIVE AT A WEST COAST INVESTMENT FIRM, MICHAEL HAD A lovely wife and three children, a comfortable salary, and a spacious home overlooking a lake. Through the witness of a business associate who introduced him to Christ, Michael's life changed dramatically. He joined a Bible study with other businessmen in the city and, with his family, became active in a local church. As he grew in his faith, Michael was committed to doing God's will for his life.

Some time later Michael left the financial world and enrolled in seminary to prepare for Christian ministry. He trusted that God would honor his decision and direct him to that special place of service. But when he graduated from seminary with honors, Michael had no clear indication of where God would have him serve. He sent out resumés to churches and Christian organizations, all to no avail. Michael began to question God's call to ministry and also to regret his decision to leave the security of the business world.

Michael found a temporary job and arranged to meet with a man he considered a soul friend, in order to process the seeming absence of God's direction in his life. Together, the two searched the Scriptures and waited upon the Lord. His friend encouraged wholehearted trust and patience as they waited for God to make plain the path. The wait turned into days, weeks, then months.

Two years later a growing denomination approached Michael about planting a church and strategizing new ministries. The position ideally suited his managerial background and vision for ministry. But those are just the surface details. A deeper understanding of the ways and workings of God came to Michael during his arduous months of seeking God, waiting, and prayer.

Today, Michael is not only in the place that seems right for him, he also shares with others the rich spiritual lessons he learned as he patiently waited for God's timetable to unfold.

Every one of us, I believe, can learn directly from Jesus the wisdom of waiting for God's timing.

The Wedding at Cana

John 2:1-11

Jesus and several disciples arrived at a marriage festival in Cana of Galilee. Mary, Jesus' mother, had already arrived. Some time into the celebration, the wine unexpectedly ran out. This would have been highly embarrassing for the host, as hospitality is incredibly important in Middle Eastern culture, and it would have been disappointing to the guests. Wine was important in a Palestinian wedding, for Psalm 104:15 (MSG) says, "God brings grain from the land, wine to make people happy."

Mary's words to Jesus, "They have no more wine," were both a state-ment of fact and a veiled request. Mary knew in her heart that her firstborn was the Son of God. She had marveled at Simeon's song at Jesus' birth (see Luke 2:29-32), heard the Baptist's teaching concerning her son (see Luke 3:16-17), and watched Jesus gather a band of disciples (see John 1:35-51). Faced with an immediate need, Mary urged Jesus to fulfill the promise of His birth by performing a miracle to replenish the wine. Given Mary's con-cern about this matter, commentators speculate that a friend or relative of Jesus was being married.

Jesus replied to Mary's request by saying, "Is that any of our business, Mother—yours or mine? This isn't my time. Don't push me" (John 2:4, MSG). When Jesus spoke about "my time" or "my hour" (see John 7:6,8,30; 8:20; 12:23,27; 13:1; 17:1), He quite likely had in mind the revelation of His glory at His Passion and Resurrection. And so Jesus initially rejected His mother's request that He miraculously replenish the wine, on the grounds that His time clearly had not yet come.

Later, Jesus' unbelieving half brothers urged an even bolder course of action. They sarcastically challenged Jesus to perform His wonders in front of the power brokers in Jerusalem: "No one who wants to become a pub-lic figure acts in secret. Since you are doing these things, show yourself to the world" (John 7:4). To this faithless suggestion Jesus replied, "For me the right time *(kairos)* has not yet come" (verse 8). The Son must patiently wait the Father's appointed time to enter Jerusalem and openly proclaim His Messiahship.

Being a godly woman, Mary recognized her untimely urging. Submitting to Jesus' divine authority, she said to the servants, "Do what-ever he tells you" (John 2:5). Even though she did not understand her son's words, Mary set aside her own will, trusting that Jesus would do the right thing in the right way at the right time.

Jesus instructed the servants to fill six stone pots with water—no small task, as each pot probably held some thirty gallons. When His task was accomplished, Jesus told them to offer the banquet master a sample. The man tasted the water drawn from the pots and was shocked. It was the finest quality wine! But only the servants knew how the wine was replenished.

What we see in Jesus' response teaches us how to handle human impatience when our will seems to be out of sync with God's timing.

Mary impatiently requested that Jesus supply the wine at the wedding feast and publicly show Himself as the Messiah. But because His "hour" had not yet come, Jesus would not be moved from His course. For this reason He declined to publicly display His glory. Instead, He patiently stayed His course, knowing He must first pursue the kingdom ministries of teaching, healing, and exorcising demons. Jesus the Son understood that He must serve patiently according to the Father's timetable.

But wait — there is a bit more in this incident to guide us.

While Jesus refused to move out of step with the Father's great plan to reveal His identity to the world at large, He remained in step with God who, through this first, silent miracle, began to unfold the plan by which He would build His spiritual kingdom on earth. For it was through this first "sign" (see verse 11) that the disciples who followed Him as an inspiring teacher (see John 1:35-51) found their faith in Jesus more deeply established. And He shows us, by His actions here, how our own faith should grow.

Jesus Ministers Spiritual Direction

FROM THIS ACCOUNT of the wedding at Cana, we learn several principles from Jesus about the ministry of spiritual direction.

He listened carefully to Mary's words.
First, we see that Jesus listened attentively to what Mary was telling Him — that is, He listened with His mind and His heart. He was attuned to Mary's expression of practical concern, and recognized her anxiety over the fact that the wedding wine was exhausted and the host would be embarrassed.

He keenly discerned God's purpose and timing.
Whereas others saw only empty water containers, Jesus grasped the Father's *kairos*—the redemptive moment when God's kingdom purpose was advancing. We see Jesus' keen sense of discernment when He said to Mary, "not yet" (verse 4), and to the servants, "now" (verse 8). Jesus did not insist on immediate "solutions" to a problem, but patiently focused on kingdom priorities.

He spoke to the situation with directness and compassion.
Armed with a clear vision of the Father's will, Jesus redirected the intention of His well-meaning but out-of-step mother. In addition, He told the servants what steps they must take to advance God's secret plan (see verses 7-8).

Ultimately, Jesus led Mary to trust God more completely. As a result of this course of action Jesus helped Mary understand that the Father was faithfully working out His purposes even when she could not make sense of the present circumstances. Though we are not told this directly in the gospel account, we can understand that Jesus' actions were intended to give Mary the confidence and courage to "hang in there" with God, even in the midst of confusion and anxiety.

One thing more: Jesus celebrated life.
For those of us who may think God is only interested in "the serious business of life" or in "ministry," Jesus' presence at the wedding feast in Cana tells us that God shows up at gatherings that are fun and full of lively celebration. Because God was present at the party, Jesus joined in the celebration with gusto. By doing so, He gave us an example of how to live balanced lives of service, prayer, family relationships, *and* recreation.

Waiting on God's Timing

WELL-INTENTIONED MARY urged her son to use His divine powers to replenish the wine that had run out. If Jesus had publicly displayed His glory so early in His ministry, God's timetable would have been short-circuited. He had disciples to train, teachings to give, and other miracles to perform. This is what Jesus meant when He said, "My time is not yet come." Lest we be too harsh with Mary for her untimely urging, though, it's hard for every one of us to see God's purpose clearly, given the busyness and confusion of our lives.

Patient waiting seems to be one of those ground rules of nature. An acorn that's forced open before it has ripened will not propagate an oak tree. A cocoon split before its time fails to yield a living butterfly. Premature births result in medical complications. Yet the ability to wait patiently does not come naturally to very many of us.

In the spiritual realm especially, it's difficult to lay aside our personal agendas and wait for God's schedule to unfold. We tend to push ahead, "take the bull by the horns," and "make things happen." We rush ahead before God, or worse, we try to force His hand. We treat God like a cosmic vending machine—drop in a dollar and expect Him to instantly deliver the objects of our desire. We're impatient for results. We want things done yesterday.

But the kingdom of God doesn't work this way. God is in no such hurry. Recall that the Lord made promises to give Abraham and Sarah a son (see Genesis 15:4); but Isaac was not born for twenty-five years, when Abraham was one hundred years old. In the Garden of Eden, God promised that Eve's offspring would crush Satan's head (see Genesis 3:15); yet the fulfillment of that promise took several thousand years to come about. Furthermore, Scripture promises that Christ's Second Coming will occur quickly: "For in just a very little while, 'He who is coming will come and will not delay'" (Hebrews 10:37); yet two thousand years have passed, and we continue to wait for Christ's return from heaven.

When God seems not to show up according to our timetable, we can nonetheless respond in several ways that move us on toward spiritual maturity.

We can trust God wholeheartedly and without reservation.

Because we as Christians have trusted God with our eternal destiny, we can surely trust Him with the concerns of this brief life. In times when God appears to be absent, depend on His unfailing goodness, faithfulness, and wisdom. What other person or power in the universe is more worthy of our confidence? In a time of confusion and stress, David said, "I trust in you, O LORD; I say, 'You are my God'" (Psalm 31:14). Like David, we can choose to believe that God is in absolute control of our lives and that He will help and answer.

We can bring our concerns to God in prayer.

Freely, honestly, we can express our needs, heartaches, and confusions to our heavenly Father. God is patient as He listens to the petitions — however misguided — of His children. He is not put off when we pour out our greatest concerns to Him. If we want to keep maturing in spirit, we will keep praying, refuse to quit, and never give up on God.

We can patiently wait on the Lord.

With dogged determination, learn to wait for God to accomplish His plans in His perfect time. The Old Testament encourages us to wait steadfastly: "Wait for the LORD; be strong and take heart and wait for the LORD" (Psalm 27:14). The New Testament directs us to be calm and firm: "be patient and stand firm, because the Lord's coming is near" (James 5:8). Those who submit to God's will and wait for His timing will receive Jesus' best gifts. As we wait, we will not be idle, for God's revealed will teaches what work needs to be done.

We can allow waiting for God to be a soul-shaping experience.
As we confidently wait upon the Lord we will find that our old limits are stretched, our soul is expanded, and our will becomes gradually aligned with God's will. Patient waiting prompts us to live in the present moment, and it develops endurance and fortitude for future tests of faith. In short, patience makes us more like Jesus (see 1 Timothy 1:16).

"When you don't know what to do, wait! God never panics and is never under pressure."[1]

A Prayer

LORD, when You seem to me to be off on another planet and when
I desperately need the sense of Your presence . . . help me to relinquish
my own agenda, and to trust You implicitly. And then, most of all, help
me to wait patiently for the unfolding of Your perfect will.

Try It Yourself

A Soul-Searching Exercise

Someone has said, "Waiting is the soil out of which dormant faith springs."
Recall an occasion when an important prayer request appeared to go
unanswered or when God seemed slow to act on your behalf.

During this test of patience were you motivated to seek God more
wholeheartedly and relinquish your will more fully?

How did this season of waiting become for you a time of purification
and strengthening?

Has it enabled you to face other times of waiting more patiently and
constructively?

Resentful and Resistant

J UDY WAS A SINGLE MOM WHO WORKED AS A HAIRDRESSER IN A TOWN
known for free thinking and even freer lifestyles. Her only exposure to
the gospel was through the wild man who shouted out Bible verses on the
street corner before sporting events. An open-minded person, Kristen
held a belief system that included bits of Buddhism, astrology, and new
age. She carried in her wallet, for some sense of guidance on how to live,
St. Francis' Prayer, which begins, "Lord, make me an instrument of your
peace. . . ."

When a friend invited Judy's daughter, Kristen, a high school junior,
to a Young Life club, Kristen loved the fun activities, the new friends, and
the talks about spiritual things. Encouraged by her school buddies, Kristen
decided to follow Christ. She signed up for a summer camp in Colorado.
At the suggestion of her club leader, Kristen joined a church where many
of her Christian friends attended. She was excited with the peace and joy
she found in God. But all this was making Judy uncomfortable.

Several months later, Kristen decided to be baptized and invited the
youth pastor to her home to get her mother's permission. Judy couldn't
contain her hostility. "Thanks, but no thanks," she said. "You want to bap-
tize my daughter, when the church is filled with hypocrites? Look at all
those televangelists who steal and sleep around!"

The young man replied, "Christians who would do such things are an
exception. Christians are not perfect, only forgiven."

"Sure, forgiven!" Judy shot back. "Christians are not the innocent
people they claim to be. Look at the Crusades, where Christians used
swords to capture the Holy Land! Look at Northern Ireland, where
Protestants and Catholics destroy the innocent with pipe bombs!"

Angrily, Judy showed the youth pastor to the door. "No daughter of
mine is going to become a narrow-minded Christian," she said.
Embarrassed, Kristen broke down in tears.

Later, though, comforted by her pastor and Christian friends, Kristen
resolved that she would continue to love her mother, and also to pray that
her resistance to the gospel would soften.

Her youth pastor also encouraged her by pointing out from Scripture
the way Jesus offered soul care to another woman who was resistant to God.

The Woman at the Well

John 4:4-30

Due to growing opposition from the Pharisees, Jesus left Judea and journeyed to Galilee. But His route was not the usual one taken by "righteous" Jews of His day.

Instead of taking the usual road through the Jordan valley, Jesus traveled right through Samaria—semi-hostile territory, given the fact that the Jews and Samaritans were enemies. About noon He came to the village of Sychar near Shechem, which was land that Jacob had given to Joseph many centuries before (see Genesis 48:22). Here in Sychar, next to Mount Gerazim—a peak sacred to the Samaritans—was Jacob's well.

Tired and thirsty, Jesus sat down beside the well for a drink while His disciples went to the village to buy food. As Jesus waited, a woman came to the well to draw water. Most women visited the well during the cool mornings and evenings, to avoid the heat of the day; this woman came at noon to avoid the scorn of the "respectable" women. The woman appears to have been unloved, rejected, wounded—a hurting child dressed up in grown woman's clothes.

Jesus began a conversation with her—and its importance can only be recognized when we understand that just by this simple engagement, Jesus was intentionally breaking down several cultural and religious barriers.

First, she was a Samaritan and He was a Jew. The Samaritans came from the intermarriage of the remnant left behind after the Assyrian deportation and foreigners introduced by the conquerors (see 2 Kings 17:23-41). Steeped in ignorance and idolatry, the Samaritans were regarded by Jews as unclean half-breeds. John added, "Jews in those days wouldn't be caught dead talking to Samaritans" (verse 9, MSG).

Second, Jesus, a Jewish spiritual leader, was speaking not only to a peasant but a peasant *woman*! Jewish religious leaders rarely spoke with women in public places. Strict rabbis taught, "Let no man talk with a woman in the street, no not with his own wife. Rather burn the words of the Law than teach them to woman."[1]

Finally, as Jesus was to discover, this particular woman was living in sin, having a series of irregular marriages. Nonetheless, He sensed a divine appointment with her, and asked, "Will you give me a drink?" (verse 7). Behind His request, though, was deep concern for the woman's soul.

When the woman replied to Jesus her response was laced with resistance expressed as *scorn*: "How come you, a Jew, are asking me, a Samaritan woman, for a drink?" (verse 9, MSG). She said, in effect, "Oh! You're sure it's all right to ask me to haul up water for you to have a drink because you're thirsty. But all the while you Jews really think we're worthless, irreligious dogs." In a way, of course, it was natural that she would scornfully project her bitterness against all Jews onto the rabbi seated before her. How many times had she been snubbed or railed at by "righteous" believers?

Ignoring her scorn, Jesus said, "If you knew the gift of God and who it is that asks you for a drink, you would have asked him and he would have given you living water" (verse 10).

Because the woman's vision was limited to temporal things, she responded with more resistance, this time expressed as *sarcasm*: "Sir, you don't even have a bucket to draw with. . . . So how are you going to get this 'living water'? Are you a better man than our ancestor Jacob, who dug this well and drank from it . . . ?" (verses 11-12, MSG). But Jesus disregarded her sarcasm as well, and explained the "living water" He offered: "Whoever drinks the water I give him will never thirst. Indeed, the water I give him will become in him a spring of water welling up to eternal life" (verse 14).

Still, the woman didn't understand Jesus' offer of a gushing fountain of spiritual life. She was fixated on her immediate, outward dilemma ("I hate coming here to draw water"). Jesus knew her problem was internal ("You're dry as the desert inside").

Once again, she responded with resistance, expressed now as *flippancy*: "Sir, give me this water so I won't ever get thirsty, won't ever have to come back to this well again!" (verse 15, MSG). Having apparently had enough of her banter, Jesus cut to the chase: "Go, call your husband" (verse 16). As the Lord directed the light of His omniscience into her heart, the woman began to squirm.

Now she responded curtly to Jesus' suggestion with resistance expressed as *evasion*: "I have no husband" (verse 17). Jesus replied, "That's nicely put: 'I have no husband.' You've had five husbands, and the man you're living with now isn't even your husband. You spoke the truth there, sure enough" (verses 17-18, MSG). As John Calvin noted, "When Jesus saw that His words were received with jeers, He applied an appropriate remedy to the disease. He struck the woman's conscience with a conviction of her sin."[2]

Arrested by Jesus' knowledge of her private world, the woman attempted to deflect attention from her sinful life by dragging the Rabbi into a debate about the proper place of worship. She expressed her resistance finally as *mockery*: "Oh, so you're a prophet! Well, tell me this: Our ancestors worshiped God at this mountain, but you Jews insist that Jerusalem is the only place for worship, right?" (verses 19-20, MSG).

Jesus ignored the woman's diversion, but told her that worship acceptable to God is determined not by place but by the attitude of one's heart. And this, finally, had an effect on the imperfect, mistreated Samaritan woman. Her resistance softened. She said, "I know that Messiah . . . is coming. When he comes, he will explain everything to us" (verse 25). Jesus brought her to the point of confessing her willingness to welcome Messiah *when he comes.*

In response to her expression of hope in the coming Messiah, Jesus boldly declared, "I am he . . . You don't have to wait any longer or look any further" (verse 26, MSG). The conversation was then interrupted, John tells us, by the returning disciples: "They were shocked. They couldn't believe he was talking with that kind of a woman. No one said what they were all thinking, but their faces showed it" (verse 27, MSG).

Leaving her water container behind, the woman hurried to town and told the people that she had found the Messiah. On the basis of the woman's testimony, many Samaritans believed in Jesus as "the Savior of the world" (verse 42).

Ephraem (d. 373), a commentator and hymn writer in the Eastern Church, wrote the following commentary about the internal progression in this Samaritan woman who parried Jesus at the well:

> At the beginning of the conversation Jesus did not make himself known to her, but first she caught sight of a thirsty man, then a Jew, then a Rabbi, afterwards a prophet, last of all the Messiah. She tried to get the better of the thirsty man, she showed dislike of the Jew, she heckled the Rabbi, she was swept off her feet by the prophet, and she adored the Christ.[3]

Jesus Ministers Spiritual Direction

JESUS' DELIBERATE ENCOUNTER with a sinful Samaritan woman gives us several insights into His ministry of spiritual direction.

Jesus ministered soul care out of a sense of divine appointment.
Scripture says, "He had *(dei)* to go through Samaria" (verse 4). The little Greek verb indicates divine necessity. From this we understand that the "chance" meeting at the well was a matter of divine design, and we see Jesus put aside His own plans and allow Himself to be led into fruitful ministry by the Spirit.

Jesus was respectful of a seeker from a different ethnic and religious background.
Jesus ministered spiritual guidance to the despised Samaritan woman with dignity, irrespective of her race and gender. He didn't look down upon the

sinful woman, but treated her with respect. Jesus crossed the divide to reconcile her world, fractured by ethnic, cultural, and gender barriers.

Jesus entered into meaningful dialogue with the woman.

"Jesus said . . . the woman said," or equivalents, occur several times in the story (see verses 7 and 9; 10 and 11; 13 and 15; 16 and 17; 19 and 21; and 25 and 26). Jesus began the dialogue with ordinary facets of life: physical thirst, a well, a husband, and so forth. Through honest dialogue Jesus gained her trust, created a safe place for her search, and challenged her to ponder spiritual realities. All the while He politely answered her questions (see verses 9,11,12) and replied to her statements (see verses 9,15,17,19,25).

Jesus skillfully discerned the woman's means of resistance and sensitively disarmed her diversions.

The Lord walked with the wounded woman through the maze of her resistance and her avoidance mechanisms, crafted to escape facing up to God's call on her life. With dignity, Jesus turned the other cheek and bore the brunt of her scorn, sarcasm, and mockery. He didn't take offense at how she spoke to Him, nor did He allow Himself to be drawn into diversionary theological debates. Rather, He brought the woman back to her basic need for relationship with God.

Jesus showed compassion and patience in dealing with the woman on her spiritual journey.

The Lord demonstrated uncommon love for the ostracized woman as He focused on the thirst of her heart. He rose above the moralistic vision of His own disciples, who were shocked that He would talk with such a woman. Jesus also treated the woman with great patience, giving her space to piece together the puzzle of life. The spiritual reorientation of a life usually takes time, and Jesus understood well the related importance of "bear[ing] patiently the bad temper of other people, the slights, the rudeness that may be offered you."[4]

Jesus did not condone the woman's behavior, but neither did He heighten her shame.

Jesus didn't lay a guilt trip on the Samaritan woman for her failed marriages and her latest illicit relationship. Prompted by the Spirit, He spoke the truth to her with directness and pointed out the better path to God.

Disarming Resistance to Relationship

THIS ENCOUNTER RAISES a number of questions:

What is spiritual resistance?

We detect in the Samaritan woman's interaction with Jesus various levels of resistance. Resistance involves an inner response that short-circuits obedience to God. Most resistance is unconscious, expressing itself as avoidance of God, reversal of a decision, or a desire to quit a commitment. Every person, somewhere along the spiritual journey, experiences resistance—some instances are small and inconsequential, others large and troublesome. As one writer put it: "We are naturally self-protective of our present sense of self and way of life."[5]

Why do people resist God?

All growth is painful. People develop pleasurable patterns of behavior, and inertia keeps them rooted in these patterns. The call to go forward with Christ challenges the pleasurable status quo, resulting in spiritual and emotional discomfort. People tend to say, "The pain I know is preferable to the unknown possibility of pain."

New teaching challenges our unconscious "grid," creating anxiety and withdrawal. Modern communication and information theory shows that a person organizes her experiences into an internal pattern or *schema*. The *schema* is the structure of our personality, formed by life experiences from childhood onward. When a person encounters new information not found in the internal pattern, she responds with resistance. For example, suppose a person has been conditioned to view God as distant and threatening. When invited to trust the loving God who is near at hand, she finds no context for this in her grid and so resists. Severe resistance, such as that of the rich young ruler, halts spiritual progress in its tracks. Moderate resistance, evident in the Samaritan woman, is a sign that the person is probing the boundaries of her current understanding. Moderate resistance "is not something to be condemned or pitied but rather welcomed as an indication that the relationship with God is broadening and deepening."[6]

The factor of sin is still at work in us. What Scripture calls "the sinful nature" (Colossians 2:11,13) resists the Spirit's call to go forward with Christ. There is something even in mature Christians that opposes God and His will. We see this in Romans 7:14-25, where the apostle Paul painfully described the resistance raised by his old nature.

How can we deal with the problem of resistance that hinders or halts spiritual progress?

Prayerfully, with the Spirit's help, identify areas of resistance. We need to clearly identify impediments to growth before they can be addressed. Through prayer and biblical reflection, invite the Spirit—whose task it is to grow souls into the image of Christ—to reveal the resistance that hinders spiritual growth.

Be humble enough to recognize that you possess limited knowledge of the spiritual life. Realize that you have much to learn about God and His ways. Be open to the possibility that your personal grid needs enlarging through new insights and experiences consistent with the Word of God. Be flexible enough to incorporate new truth about God and His ways into your interpretive grid.

Catch a vision for new spiritual possibilities that God offers you. Caught between maintaining the status quo and experiencing spiritual growth, explore your spiritual hunger for God. Even when stuck in the doldrums, most of us long for a closer relationship with Christ. Speak honestly with God about your deepest spiritual aspirations. Talk about these desires with a spiritually sensitive friend.

If the resistance is caused by dark spiritual forces, seek out competent spiritual counsel. Share your struggle with a pastor or gifted friend who will prayerfully uphold you in the battle for your soul. Unreservedly trust the Lord, and you will find strength to resist the Devil and journey forward with Christ.

When encountering resistance, remember that progress in the spiritual life will be proportional to the extent to which you surrender your will and interests to God. It is a spiritual axiom that the Lord works in our life to the degree that we give Him permission to do so (consider Proverbs 3:5-6; Hebrews 11:6).

A PRAYER

LORD, You know how I follow the path of least resistance, even if it means withdrawing myself from Your loving presence. By Your Spirit grant the grace that will enable me to break through each of my stubborn means of resistance so that I may cling tightly to You.

TRY IT YOURSELF

1. Ask God to help you minister to a resistant soul.

Identify a friend who appears to be resisting God and who is willing to share, in confidence, his inner world with you. Prayerfully discern how the Spirit is working in this person's life.

2. Ask God to help you recognize ways this person is resisting God's call upon his life.

Can you identify what avoidance mechanisms might be at work—repression, denial, intellectualizing, or displacing emotions or feelings (like guilt, anger, or fear) to another object? As led by the Spirit, gently explore with your friend his means of resistance to relationship.

Loss of Passion for Life

DALE IS A CHRISTIAN LEADER WITH THIRTY YEARS OF MINISTRY EXPERI-
ence. Three years ago his only son was killed in an automobile acci-
dent involving a drunk driver. Both Dale and his wife, Suzie, were
devastated by the loss of their beloved son. Six months later Suzie became
ill, but the doctors thought her condition was easily treatable.
Unfortunately, her condition was misdiagnosed, and within a few weeks
she passed away.

Dale took his wife's death very hard. Physically, his body ached most
of the time. He was exhausted but couldn't sleep. He was hungry but
couldn't eat. Socially, he withdrew from people. He didn't read the mail or
the many sympathy cards that piled up.

For months he experienced anger toward God for the death of his
beloved family. Spiritually, Dale lost the sense of God's presence. He had
sunk into a deep rut of depression that immobilized every aspect of his
being.

One day, a friend who was also a pastor showed up at Dale's door.
"Come on," he said, "we're going to the health club to work out." Dale
didn't even have the will to protest. At the gym, the two men ran on the
treadmill and pumped iron. At the end of their workout they wound up
soaking in the hot tub, where the friend encouraged Dale to talk—and
gradually, Dale put words to his painful feelings and angry reactions to
God.

This was the beginning of Dale's recovery. Later, a friend invited him
to become part of a small group where he could be supported with love and
care. But the turning point for Dale occurred at a weekend retreat with
men who had experienced similar devastating losses. Following a small
group session, one man gave Dale a big hug. The physical hug touched him
profoundly at the emotional level, giving flesh to the healing work God was
slowly doing inside him. From that point on, Dale's anger softened to sadness, which gradually turned to peace. He was on the road back to life.

Jesus, too, encountered people whose lives lay about them in ruins,
people who needed His soul care to move them out of the deep ruts of
despair they'd sunk into. One such man was an invalid, whom Jesus met
beside the healing pool of Bethesda.

The Invalid at Bethesda

John 5:1-15

Jesus was in Jerusalem for a feast of the Jews. Near the Sheep Gate was a spring-fed pool called Bethesda, meaning "house of mercy," and it was surrounded by five pillared porches. Many blind, lame, and paralyzed people reclined there. Archeologists tell us the pool was 55 feet long by 12 feet wide, and accessed by stone stairs. The mineral water that filled the pool was fed by a spring that bubbled up intermittently. Essentially, Bethesda was a super health spa in its day. It was popularly believed that a sick person who entered the pool when the mineral water was flowing would be healed of her illness.

The Invalid's Predicament

Among those lying by the pool was a man who had been an "invalid" for thirty-eight years. He suffered from a "weakness" or "infirmity" *(astheneia)* that prevented him from entering the healing waters. Jesus approached the colonnade, saw the poor man lying there, and capably discerned the invalid's real problem. It's revealed in the question Jesus asked the man—a question meant to kindle his interest and test his will: "Do you want to get well?" (verse 6).

In reply, the invalid slowly raised his head and said to Jesus with a weak voice, "I have no one to help me into the pool when the water is stirred. While I am trying to get in, someone else goes down ahead of me" (verse 7).

Jesus seems to have eyed the stranger in front of Him and gauged his response.

The Invalid's Healing

To everyone's surprise, Jesus extended His hand to the man and gave him the *command*, "Get up! Pick up your mat and walk" (verse 8). In effect Jesus was saying, "You don't need to live with this paralyzing condition. Do the thing you have to do." And so He gave the man the first condition for his healing: Make the conscious choice to pick up your mat.

The story continues, "At once the man was cured; he picked up his mat and walked" (verse 9). For the first time in decades the invalid stood, unaided, on his own two feet. Yet he didn't know who the man was that healed him (see verses 11,13).

Later, Jesus went to the temple where He found the man giving thanks to God for his healing. Jesus approached the man and said, "Stop sinning or something worse may happen to you" (verse 14). Clearly, suffering and sickness are not always the result of personal sin (see John 9:2-3), but in this case, the man's "paralysis" was somehow related to sin in his life. Perhaps he'd harbored years of chronic bitterness over what had befallen him.

The Invalid's Issue

What *had* immobilized the poor man, causing him to lie helplessly by the pool for thirty-eight years? He may have suffered a debilitating physical condition. Perhaps, when through the years no one came to help him into the pool (see verse 7), he became bitter and resentful—and maybe even guilt-ridden for having these feelings (see verse 14). In essence, it seems this man had resigned himself to his infirmity and had lost hope. The Bible commentator B. F. Westcott wrote, "It might seem that [the invalid] acquiesced in his condition, and was unwilling to make any vigorous effort to gain relief."[1]

There is another possibility, of course. It's possible that many years before, the man had simply grown comfortable with making his living by begging. Travel to any country today, even major U.S. cities, and you find people who have become "professional" beggars. Some long ago stopped using their God-given skills or gifts, because they found it easier to trade on the generosity and sympathy of other people.

Whatever the case, the man had long ago reconciled himself to his condition. He may have said, "I can't help myself. This is the way I am. This is the way God meant me to be." Mistrusting God's love and care, he lost the will to get up and get on with his life.

Jesus Ministers Spiritual Direction

THE STORY OF Jesus' encounter with the invalid at the pool of Bethesda offers insights into our Lord's ministry of spiritual direction to a needy stranger.

Jesus seized the initiative to minister to the man in his affliction.

The invalid didn't ask Jesus for help; rather, the Lord on His own initiative came to the aid of one in pain. Jesus knew his need and reached out with mercy and compassion. As G. Campbell Morgan put it, "He saw, He knew, He acted."[2] Sheer goodness and mercy moved Jesus to bless the poor man languishing in misery.

Jesus gained an opening into the invalid's life by a probing question.

By the simple but arresting question "Do you want to get well?" Jesus prodded the man out of his apathy and resignation—a condition that blocked the faith and action necessary for his cure. Jesus' question also kindled in the man a spark of hope for a new beginning.

Jesus practiced directive spiritual guidance.

The Lord confronted the man's problem head-on. He was proactive in telling the "invalid" the difficult things he must do. He must take concrete steps as conditions of his healing. He must rise from the ground, pick up his sleeping mat, and begin to walk in the right direction. Jesus' spiritual guidance was directive as well as nondirective.

Jesus instructed the man in God's revealed will from the Bible.
The Lord said, "Stop sinning or something worse may happen to you" (verse 14). Jesus brought to the man's attention a crucial biblical principle relevant to his condition—he must cease the sinful behavior pattern that contributed to his immobility. Teaching at the strategic moments of need is an important component of spiritual direction.

Moving Beyond Apathy

THOUGH IT MAY be hard to admit, we—like the invalid at Bethesda—may choose to cling to our weaknesses, and sometimes even to our illnesses. We just will not allow ourselves to be helped. Being "victims" gets us some benefit, brings us some satisfaction; otherwise we wouldn't cling to a weak, hurting, and broken identity. Perhaps this was part of the invalid's real spiritual problem.

Many of us are "invalids" in the way we approach life. We don't "stir up" our God-given gifts and talents; we don't enter the "callings" God has coded into us at birth, we don't walk in the works God has prepared for us to do. As a result, we are far from the path that would lead us to spiritual wholeness—to a life of spiritual passion, joy, and meaningful service to God and man.

These and other interior motives weaken and diminish a healthy spirit, until it is atrophied like an unused muscle. By allowing our passion for living to be lost, we become listless and apathetic. Slowly, we cease caring about God, others, or life itself.

This is a condition known to the ancients—among them John Cassian (d. 435), John Climacus (d. 649), and Thomas Aquinas (d. 1274)—as *acedia*, from a Greek word meaning "not caring." This is a serious malady, horribly debilitating to our Christian walk.

What is acedia?
Acedia is a state of fatigue, involving apathy ("I couldn't care less") and loss of passion for life. It's a condition of spiritual sluggishness and joylessness, the "dry and withered" condition described in Psalm 90:6. Acedia is reflected in the psalmist's lament, "my sad life's dilapidated, a falling-down barn" (Psalm 119:28, MSG). Christian theologians identified acedia as one of eight evil passions: gluttony, fornication, greed, anger, despair, acedia,

vainglory, and pride. Others cited acedia as one of the seven capital sins.

Renewed attention is being paid today to the spirit of acedia. Lethargy, fatal resignation, and loss of spiritual passion are common maladies in the Western world—even in the church, which ought to be overflowing with joy and longing for God.

What causes loss of passion for life?

Because we humans are created a body–soul–spirit unity, acedia might be caused by many physical, emotional, or spiritual factors. A nagging physical illness can drag body and spirit into fatigue. Emotional exhaustion can depress the soul into listlessness. But a major cause of acedia is spiritual neglect, any form of which erodes passion for God. Clinging to unconfessed sins also robs the soul of vitality and joy. Some cherished sin likely dried up the invalid's soul and paralyzed his desire to get well.

What are acedia's effects?

The spirit of acedia is the spirit of sadness, indifference, and apathy. A heart so afflicted has little desire for life or for God. Acedia has been called a capital sin because it is the "head," or root cause, of many daughter vices— impure thoughts and actions that promise immediate satisfaction. Acedia often leads to inactivity, discouragement, and depression.[3]

How might one move from apathy to recapture holy desire for God?

If sin is the immediate cause of acedia, lance the poisonous boil. To dispel spiritual apathy and its cancerous cousins, face up to the vices in your life. Admit the besieging sin, call it by name, understand and feel the damage it has caused, and confess it to God. Allow the healing power of God to enter the wounded, painful places. A spiritual, like a physical, wound must be diagnosed, cleaned, and then protected. Jesus' command to the invalid, "Stop sinning," attacked the root that fed his lethargy.

Take a first practical step toward restoration. Only God's grace can break the power of sin; but we must do our part (see Philippians 2:12-13). Lay aside excuses and change the sinful behavior pattern. In dependence on God, get off the floor and take a first step in the right direction. "Take courage, . . . and may the LORD be with those who do what is right" (2 Chronicles 19:11, NLT). Ask a friend to take your hand and pray with you. If possible, lend a hand to someone in need; helping another will get your mind off yourself and lift your spirit.

Recapture hope in God. Hope is the antidote to indifference and despair. Scripture promises, "Those who hope in the LORD will renew their strength. They will soar on wings like eagles; they will run and not grow weary, they will walk and not be faint" (Isaiah 40:31). The writer of Hebrews tells us that hope is "an anchor for the soul" (Hebrews 6:19), renewing the life with vitality. Allow joyful hope to supplant sorrowful resignation.

Rekindle relationship with Christ. Prayerfully nurture holy longing for Christ. The psalmist mused: "Whom have I in heaven but you? And earth has nothing I desire besides you. My flesh and my heart may fail, but God is the strength of my heart and my portion forever" (Psalm 73:25-26). As Kenneth Boa expresses it well:

> Without holy desire we will succumb to the sin of spiritual acedia, or indifference, apathy, and boredom. People who lose the sharp edge of intention and calling can slip into a morass of listlessness and feelings of failure. We must often ask God for the grace of acute desire so that we will hunger and thirst for him.[4]

Live a balanced life of work and prayer. St. Benedict (d. 543) pointed out that the rhythm of prayer and labor *(ora et labora)* promotes spiritual passion. Prayer dispels dark powers and opens the heart to renewing grace. Manual labor (see 1 Thessalonians 4:11; 2 Thessalonians 3:8,10; Ephesians 4:28) renews physical and spiritual energy. Through the rhythm of prayer, work, and recreation, our spirits are refreshed. An overload of spiritual exercises can produce soul weariness as well. James Stalker remarks, "Religious exercises were never intended to absorb the whole of our time but to supply strength for the discharge of duty in the family and in the market-place; the attempt to override nature cannot but have its revenge."[5]

A PRAYER

LORD, the world, my flesh, and the Devil conspire to drain life from my soul. Empower me to pursue You through renewing disciplines that will keep the recreative and empowering life of Your Spirit flowing through my soul—a soul susceptible to discontent and dejection.

TRY IT YOURSELF

Recapture lost desire.

Reflect on your spiritual journey, perhaps by reading entries from your journal. Identify a time of life in which you lost holy desire for God and became indifferent or apathetic.

Older authorities described a chain of sinful passions and noted that each passion is fed by the previous one up the chain. John Cassian wrote, "From an excess of gluttony there inevitably springs fornication;

from fornication, greed; from greed, anger; from anger, sadness; and from sadness, acedia."[6] The progression looks like this:

Gluttony ➡ Fornication ➡ Greed ➡ Anger ➡ Sadness ➡ Acedia

Have you been trapped by any one of these sins that breed spiritual lethargy? How did you rekindle passion for God?

If you are currently stuck in spiritual apathy, how might this chapter help you rekindle passion for life and holy desire for God?

Captivated by Experience

MONICA IS A CAREER WOMAN WHO HAS HUNGERED FOR A DEEPER relationship with Christ. Her friend Sarah suggested that the two of them participate in a spiritual-life workshop at a Christian retreat center known for its communal and spiritual vitality. Through the years, Sarah assured her, many have had life-changing encounters with Christ there, and others have found healing for emotional and spiritual wounds. Even so, Monica felt a little uncertain, because she'd never been to a retreat center before.

When the two friends arrived at the center, Monica was very pleasantly surprised. Through informative teachings on the spiritual life, times of prayer, and quiet walks in nature, she met God through encounters of grace. During the retreat, her soul was uplifted and God became marvelously real. So much so that Monica returned to the retreat center the following year. Once again the Holy Spirit brought her "up the mountain," where she experienced the love and beauty of the Lord. Monica had found a renewing and empowering spiritual home. At the end of her second trip, she looked forward to meeting God in life-changing ways the next year in this sacred place.

Back at home, Monica began a monthly prayer meeting and served as a spiritual director to three other women. She was now helping others grow in Christ.

One day Monica received a letter saying that, due to financial considerations, the retreat center was closing its doors. This wonderful place where Monica found soul-captivating encounters with God would no longer be there. She felt a deep sense of loss. Where would she find another such place that could give her the mountaintop experiences with God that replenished her within and strengthened her for ministering to others?

Jesus' Transfiguration

Matthew 17:1-9; Mark 9:2-9; Luke 9:28-36
It was in Caesarea Philippi that Peter recognized who Jesus was, confessing, "You are the Christ" (Matthew 16:16). A week later, the Lord led him and two other disciples—James and John—up the slopes of a high mountain, quite possibly the nearby 9,400-foot Mount Hermon. During the evening

hours Jesus devoted Himself to prayer, and as it grew dark the disciples dozed off. As Jesus was praying, suddenly "he was transfigured before them" (Matthew 17:2). The verb *metamorphoō* (from which comes our word *metamorphosis*) indicates that Jesus' deity, veiled since His birth, shone forth in fierce glory. His face radiated like the sun, and His clothes glistened dazzling white, like lightning. In the darkness of the mountain night, it must have been an electrifying sight.

While the three disciples were still catching their breath, Moses and Elijah appeared from heaven and talked with Jesus. These twin towers of the old order—Israel's great Law-receiver and the representative of the great prophets—"spoke about his departure [*exodos*], which he was about to bring to fulfillment at Jerusalem" (Luke 9:31). In language recalling Israel's exodus from Egypt, Moses and Elijah dialogued with Jesus about His coming death and resurrection.

Shaken, Peter blurted out, "Rabbi, it is good for us to be here. Let us put up three shelters—one for you, one for Moses and one for Elijah" (Mark 9:5). Because the Feast of Tabernacles was at hand, Peter must have thought that building booths was in order, in an attempt to celebrate the Feast there on the mountain. Fixated on this private preview of the kingdom, the disciples likely wanted to keep Jesus, Moses, and Elijah in place. Peter, especially, seems to have wanted to "hang out" on the mountain and prolong this glorious scene. We could say he was looking for God in a place, not in the person of Jesus.

But God interrupted Peter's plan: "While [Peter] was still speaking, a bright cloud enveloped them, and a voice from the cloud said, 'This is my Son, whom I love; with him I am well pleased. Listen to him!'" (Matthew 17:5). The cloud that enveloped the mountain recalls the cloud that covered Mount Sinai at the giving of the Law—the cloud from which God spoke to Moses (see Exodus 24:15-18). The cloud was the Shekinah glory, the visible presence of God. The heavenly voice certified to the disciples that Jesus was indeed God's Son.

Now the disciples fell on their faces, stunned. Jesus told them to rise up and not be afraid. When the men looked up, Moses and Elijah were gone, and "They saw no one except Jesus" (Matthew 17:8). The great representatives of the old order vanished, leaving only the One who would inaugurate the New Covenant.

As they came down the mountain, still in shock from their encounter with the glory of God in Christ, the three men were given a directive that must have been a bit disappointing and confusing. Jesus instructed them not to disclose what they had seen . . . at least until His exodus from this world was accomplished.

What was the purpose, they may have wondered, in allowing them to have such a marvelous experience . . . and then forbidding them to focus on it?

Jesus Ministers Spiritual Direction

WHEN WE HUNGER for vibrant encounters with God—and most of us do—Jesus has wise direction to offer us.

He discerned the spiritual needs of His disciples.
Jesus knew that His followers had failed to understand what He was about. He'd recently shared with them the importance and absolute need for Him to suffer and die (see Matthew 16:21); but they'd wrongly concluded that His death would be the end of His mission. To correct their misunderstanding, Jesus led this small inner circle of disciples up the mountain to witness not only the Father placing a "seal of approval" on His Son and His mission of suffering, but to view a glimpse of His eternal nature, as well.

One of their real needs, and ours, was to know that Christ is God eternally present with us.

Jesus ministered with tenderness and affection.
During the week before the Transfiguration, Peter and Jesus had been involved in a dispute. Peter had taken Jesus aside and rebuked Him for suggesting that He must suffer and die (see Matthew 16:22). Jesus responded by strongly rebuking Peter, calling him a tool of Satan (see verse 23). In spite of this tension, Jesus didn't grind Peter into the dust when he fell flat on his face on the mountain. Rather, Jesus approached Peter and the others and tenderly touched them. (So often during His ministry, Jesus consoled and strengthened people by a loving touch. See Matthew 8:3,15; 9:25,29; 17:7; Luke 22:51).

Awed and cowed by the radiance of Christ's divinity, the disciples needed to be comforted by the touch of His humanity.

He offered reassurance and encouragement.
Overwhelmed by God's awesome holiness and their own sin, the disciples' hearts were filled with fright. As the Scripture says, "It is a dreadful thing to fall into the hands of the living God" (Hebrews 10:31). Jesus encouraged the fear-stricken disciples with the comforting words, "Don't be afraid" (Matthew 17:7).

As is always the case, their hearts were strengthened when, lifting their eyes, they saw Jesus alone and allowed Him to fill their field of vision.

In counterbalance to this awesome "experience," Jesus offered clear, practical directives.

Jesus allowed the disciples the freedom to take in what they'd seen and heard on the holy mountain. But this was to be more than an "experience." There were some directives to be dealt with.

Jesus corrected their failure to understand the necessity of His death for the sins of the world. He also told the disciples what they must do: They must get up from the ground and renounce fear (see Matthew 17:7), and they were not to tell anyone what they'd seen until He had risen from the dead (verse 9).

Managing the Mountaintop

GOD GAVE PETER, James, and John a glorious vision to strengthen them for the coming days when they would experience terror, doubt, and inner conflict. But they were so captivated by the "peak" experience that it became their focus. They wanted to preserve this awesome vision of God. How disappointed the three were when Jesus led them down the mountain. They had become fixed on the experience, rather than on God's larger purpose for their lives. Even though their motives were muddled, the disciples' encounter with God's glory on the mountain became an anchor for the rest of their days. The Transfiguration was a memorial stone, an Ebenezer they would never forget (see 1 Samuel 7:12).

John cherished that meeting with God, for years later he wrote, "We have seen his glory, the glory of the One and Only, who came from the Father, full of grace and truth" (John 1:14). And many years after the Transfiguration Peter likewise wrote, "we were eyewitnesses of his majesty. For he [Christ] received honor and glory from God the Father when the voice came to him from the Majestic Glory, saying, 'This is my Son, whom I love; with him I am well pleased.' We ourselves heard this voice that came from heaven when we were with him on the sacred mountain" (2 Peter 1:16-18).

Like Monica in the opening story, and like these three disciples, you and I may also want to hang onto the glory of our spiritual "mountaintop" experiences. We may mourn when God calls us from the heights back down to the valley floor of everyday living.

How can we manage the mountaintop experience in a way that pleases God?

We can accept that a God-given mountaintop experience is significant.

Gerald May notes that spiritual journeys often begin with a dramatic spiritual experience (for example, Moses, Cornelius, Saul/Paul), and the special encounter often becomes an occasion for insight, encouragement, and growth.[1]

God often gives such an experience that we might see Him more clearly and love Him more dearly.

If God has graced you with a significant spiritual vision, savor the experience and store it away in your memory bank. Erect your Ebenezer — your altar of remembrance — and be prepared to move on.

We can release the experience . . . and keep the joy.

God, it seems, does not allow our encounters with His glory to last very long . . . and for very good reason. His awesome glory is blinding. The reality is that "Too clear a manifestation of God, even though it related to Jesus, would rather overpower than empower us."[2]

Yes, the rhythm of the spiritual journey involves occasional ascents up the mountain followed by descents to the plain below. No journey moves from peak to peak alone. Attempts to hold onto an awe-filled experience amount to reasserting control over our life — and control is a deadly enemy of spiritual growth.

Wisely, John of the Cross wrote, "Delightful feelings do not of themselves lead the soul to God, but rather cause it to become attached to delightful feelings."[3]

We can reflect on the important question, "What would God have me do with this experience?"

Allow the grace of the mountaintop to mold you into the person God intends you to be. Determine what new passion has been stirred up in you by the Spirit. Ask how this grace might be used to advance Christ's kingdom. We must not allow ourselves to fixate on the experience itself.

As Barclay explains, "The moment of glory does not exist for its own sake; it exists to clothe the common things with a sheen and a radiance they never had before."[4]

We can return to the practical demands of living and serving in the real world.

Jesus led the disciples from the glory and luxury of the mountain to the pain and routine of the valley. After the dazzling encounter with the Shekinah glory, Jesus and His men returned to a scene of human misery and need (Matthew 9:14-27). Let's face it, "The Mount of Transfiguration is always more enjoyable than either the daily ministry or the way of the Cross."[5]

As disciples of Jesus Christ, we too must follow the Lord's example by ministering to a lost and hurting world.

A PRAYER

LORD, I am tempted to become transfixed with the radiance of Your glory and so lose sight of the unsurpassing worth of Your Person. Help me to seek after, love, and worship You rather than become fixed on fleeting experiences, however alluring.

TRY IT YOURSELF

1. Use this reflective exercise.

Prayerfully recall a time in which God blessed you with a significant "mountaintop" spiritual experience.

2. Consider these questions:

Looking back, can you discern the purpose for which God gave you that grace at that particular time in your journey?

How have your life and service been affected by that experience?

How would you respond differently if you should be favored with a similar grace in the future?

Guilt-Ridden

THE CHILD OF DIVORCED PARENTS, CATHY MOVED TO THE WEST COAST after high school graduation. After living under her parents' "overprotective eye," as she called it, she was sure "freedom" was going to be great.

Although Cathy considered herself to be a moderately devout Christian, she'd never really thought of abstinence as that big a deal. Among her new West Coast friends, abstinence was something of a joke. And so Cathy was soon involved in a series of sexual liaisons . . . which led to a pregnancy. When her boyfriend pressured her to get an abortion she was unsure. But given her inability to support the child, she reluctantly consented.

Following the abortion, however, Cathy was overcome with anxiety and guilt. In a few weeks she slid downhill into depression. At first, she thought the negative mood would ease with time, but the stress and guilt continued to build. After two months, she was sunk in depression's depths.

Even though she was desperate to talk to someone, Cathy couldn't muster the will to tell her family about the abortion. And though she was still active in her church, she felt she'd committed the "unpardonable sin." Now she was sure that God would not—or *could* not—forgive her for ending the life of a child. Several months after the abortion she began to drink heavily to dull the pain. Her life was falling apart under the weight of all her guilt. At a Christian pregnancy center Cathy received counseling and joined a support group. Here she was finally able to confess her wrongdoing and begin to grieve over the life that was taken.

In time, a deep sense of peace came over her soul, as guilt evaporated, little by little, in the depths of God's love and forgiving grace.

Jon's story is quite different. He was raised in a Christian home where, unfortunately, faultless performance was demanded and strict discipline was administered. Jesus' words were interpreted with absolute finality: "Be perfect . . . as your heavenly Father is perfect" (Matthew 5:48). The lack of a grace-filled environment took a heavy toll on the young man in his adolescent years and beyond.

When Jon fell short of this legalistic standard, guilt stabbed at his heart. To ward off these feelings, he strove to be perfect at school and on the sports field. His repeated failure to rise to this perfect performance bar led him to believe that God could never accept him as he was. And so his teen years were filled with tremendous guilt and shame, though he prayed to accept Christ a hundred times, trying to lay hold of a God who continually eluded him. In his case, it was *false* guilt that blocked his ability to receive God's love.

Jon's first pastorate was ineffective. He saw a spiritual counselor who helped him understand that he had internalized the voice of the Pharisee, who said, "Live up to the letter of the law or be lost." His was a religion by measurement of right and wrong behavior. Like a heavy millstone on his back, the curse of legalism crushed Jon's spirit.

The counselor also helped Jon understand that God has clothed him with the righteousness of Christ, and that God does not expect faultless perfection, but reliance on His grace to cover him when he does sin. In the months that followed, Jon's tormenting guilt gradually gave way to a sense of God's love and peace.

Like these two guilt-ridden people, every one of us needs the kind of soul care Jesus offers to deal with guilt's crippling effects.

The Woman Taken in Adultery

John 8:1-11

After the Feast of Tabernacles, Jesus spent the night on the Mount of Olives. The next morning in the temple court He taught worshippers who lingered after the feast.[1] As He was speaking, some scribes and Pharisees dragged a woman before Him, saying, "Teacher, this woman was caught in the act of adultery" (verse 4). They added, "In the Law Moses commanded us to stone such women. Now what do you say?" (verse 5).

Adultery was indeed a serious offense under Jewish law. But these Jewish authorities had bent the Law, which states that *both* the offending man and woman should be condemned (see Leviticus 20:10; Deuteronomy 22:22).

Defending the Law was not their primary focus, we see, as the account continues: "They were using this question as a trap, in order to have a basis for accusing him" (verse 6). The teachers of the Law and the Pharisees had no intention of restoring the woman, only of using her as a pawn to ensnare Jesus. If Jesus recommended mercy, they could accuse Him of breaking the Law of Moses. If Jesus recommended justice by stoning, they could accuse Him of violating Roman law that forbid the Jews from executing capital punishment (see John 18:31). Undoubtedly, they thought they had Jesus boxed into a corner. How would He get Himself out of this dilemma?

Without saying a word, Jesus bent down and wrote on the ground with His finger. Instead of responding to their question, Jesus "answered" with the silence of His divine authority—even as Yahweh had written the tablets of the Law with His finger (see Exodus 31:18). And on a very practical level, by remaining silent He shifted attention from the woman to Himself. One thing more: By bending down, Jesus the sinless One, put Himself on the same level as the guilt-ridden woman who was crouched shamefully on the ground.

But what did Jesus write in the dust? The verb used in Scripture for "write," *katagraphō* (verse 6), in Greek means to "write against" or "accuse." I suspect that Jesus wrote a commandment that confronted the Jewish authorities with their own sin.

When the authorities continued to question Jesus, He stood up and said to them, "If any one of you is without sin, let him be the first to throw a stone at her" (verse 7). The Law prescribed that the judging witnesses must be innocent themselves (see Deuteronomy 19:16-19) and that they should cast the first stones (see Deuteronomy 13:9; 17:7). Knowing the immoral thoughts and actions of these Jewish authorities, Jesus turned the charge back upon them.

Then for the second time, Jesus bent down and wrote on the ground. Some suggest that He wrote from Exodus 23:7, which in effect says, "Refrain from a false matter, and leave the judgment to God." Something like this must have occurred because, stung with a sense of their own guilt, the accusers turned and slunk away, one at a time. The temple court was empty except for the sinless prophet and the sinful woman. As Augustine elegantly put it, "There remained only two: a great misery and a great pity."[2]

Now when Jesus rose to His feet again, He turned to the accused and asked, "Woman, where are they? Has no one condemned you?" (verse 10). No self-appointed judge remained to condemn the adulteress—and neither did Jesus accuse her (though He was the only One perfect to do so). The compassion and grace in His words enabled the woman to grasp for the first time that her offense was forgivable.

We can well imagine that the woman's face began to beam: "No, Lord," she said (verse 11, NLT)—words that affirmed her faith in Jesus' authority to forgive sins.

Jesus replied, "Then neither do I condemn you."

The episode ends with Jesus saying, "Go now and leave your life of sin" (verse 11). While quick to forgive, the Lord directed the woman to leave her immoral ways and walk uprightly before God. The woman who had been dragged before Jesus . . . an adulteress, in shame . . . went away forgiven, a new creature in Christ.

Jesus Ministers Spiritual Direction

IN JESUS' ENCOUNTER with self-righteous authorities, and with a sinful woman, we can learn important principles of spiritual direction for ourselves.

First, let's consider His dealings with the scribes and Pharisees:

Jesus dealt firmly with the vindictive religious authorities.

The scribes and Pharisees set a trap for Jesus and thought they'd caught Him on the horns of an insoluble dilemma. But with strength of purpose, the Lord led them into the very trap they'd set for Him. He preserved the integrity of God's Law, while spoiling the evil designs of His hypocritical accusers.

Jesus used the power of selective silence to lay bare their hearts.

The story is told of a young woman who came with a problem to the famous psychologist Carl Rogers. For several sessions they sat together in silence, and after a few visits the woman was much improved. At the exit interview the woman said to Dr. Rogers, "Thank you for helping me so much."

Jesus wisely knew when to say nothing so as to create space for the Spirit's convicting work in the hearts of the self-righteous. Jesus spoke sparingly; but when He spoke His words had powerful effect.

The Lord applied the Word of God in the power of the Spirit to disarm His accusers.

Jesus knew the requirements of the law, both Roman law and Jewish law. He directed a telling text of Scripture to the Jewish authorities that uncovered their sins and sent them scurrying to the shadows. The scribes and Pharisees were defenseless against the power of the Word of God applied with *true* righteousness.

Now let's consider Jesus' reaction to the woman:

Jesus provided her with a safe haven in which to wrestle with her moral issues.

The woman was at grave risk in the hands of the conniving religious authorities of the day. The only place in the universe where she was absolutely safe was with Jesus. In His presence she found the grace to face her destructive behavior.

Jesus demonstrated unconditional acceptance of the woman as the valued image of God.

The Lord dealt with the woman on the basis of her God-given dignity rather than in terms of the accusation brought against her. Jesus inferred that behavior (what a person does) does not define personhood (who a person is). His acceptance of her intrinsic worth affirmed her in her moral struggle.

Jesus' primary emotion toward this sinful woman was pity, not condemnation.

The Lord's overriding intention was to restore the erring person, not to humiliate or destroy her. Consider the contrast in motives: "The scribes and Pharisees . . . knew the thrill of exercising power to condemn; Jesus knows the thrill of exercising power to forgive. Jesus regarded the sinner with pity born of love."[3]

Jesus ministered spiritual direction with gentleness and compassion.

Whereas Jesus dealt firmly with the self-righteous authorities, He dealt gently with the sin-chastened woman. He addressed the adulteress with the same endearing word *(gynai)* that He spoke to His mother at Cana (see John 2:4) and later from the cross (see John 19:26). The Lord's manner of dealing with the sinful woman reflects what Paul later described as the "meekness and gentleness of Christ" (2 Corinthians 10:1).

Jesus answered law with grace and mingled justice with mercy.

Jesus maintained a righteous balance between uncovering the sin and forgiving the sinner. He demonstrated that God gives repentant sinners a second (and a third!) chance to repent and walk uprightly before Him. Jesus showed "that the mechanical and rigorous administration of laws, however lofty the ideals they employ, is not, in the last resort, the best way of dealing with sinners as persons, particularly when the administrators cannot be expected to have perfectly clean hands."[4]

Jesus called for decisive amendment of her life.

The Lord commanded the forgiven adulteress, "Go now and leave your life of sin." A condition for receiving God's forgiveness is that we turn from the conduct that seared the soul with guilt. From then on, she was to live a righteous life. Which is to say, Jesus offered tough love rather than cheap grace.

Casting Off the Burden of Guilt

AT TIMES, EACH of us is overcome with a sense of guilt that gnaws relentlessly at our souls.

A man was preaching atop a box in London's Hyde Park. Pointing to passers-by he cried out, "Guilty! Guilty!" Some people looked at him with curiosity; others turned away with embarrassment. But one man was heard to say to a friend, "How did he find out?"

What is this thing called guilt?

Guilt takes two forms: true guilt and false guilt. A person experiences true guilt when he does something wrong or has not done what is right. Sin creates a disturbing distance between God and the offending soul. True guilt, sometimes called healthy guilt, checks the spread of evil and points the soul back to God. True guilt is not without its pain. According to Psalm 38, guilt produced psychosomatic symptoms (see verses 3-7), troubled David's mind (see verses 8-9), and robbed his zest for life (see verses 13-14).

False, or unhealthy, guilt arises from listening to the condemning voice of the Pharisee within. It's caused by heeding the lie that says we gain God's favor by living up to the bar of absolute perfection. The reality is that "we all stumble in many ways" (James 3:2). Perfection will be achieved only when believers see Christ at His coming (see 1 John 3:2).

Another way to put it is that false guilt is all about *feeling* guilty without *being* guilty. Some Christians know that their sins are forgiven, but their feelings betray this. C. S. Lewis said that the Devil loves to torment Christians with "that vague cloud of unspecified guilt."[5] False guilt blocks the sense of God's presence, hinders prayer, and retards spiritual growth.

Henri Nouwen wrote:

One of the greatest challenges of the spiritual life is to receive God's forgiveness. There is something in us humans that keeps us clinging to our sins and prevents us from letting God erase our past and offer us a completely new beginning. Sometimes it even seems as though I want to prove to God that my darkness is too great to overcome . . . Receiving forgiveness requires a total willingness to let God be God and do all the healing, restoring, and renewing.[6]

How does a person shake the guilt that torments the soul and spirit?

A first step is to realize that we can't silence the condemning voice by our own resources. Consider the following:

God erases true guilt when the offender confesses the fault and turns from it. The solution to true guilt is to repent of the root sin and rest in the biblical verdict that *God forgives.* Yahweh described himself to Moses as: "The LORD, the LORD, the compassionate and gracious God . . . abounding in love and faithfulness, maintaining love to thousands, and forgiving wickedness, rebellion and sin" (Exodus 34:6-7). God's major job description is to forgive the sin we confess and to erase its guilt.

God erases false guilt as the repentant accepts His grace and avoids the peril of legalism. The all-knowing Judge declares Christians who have confessed their sins "Not guilty!" When you sin and feel the pang of remorse, remember the Cross of Christ and forgive yourself, even as the Father has forgiven you. As Paul wrote, "There is now no condemnation for those who are in Christ Jesus" (Romans 8:1). Go to Jesus and claim His forgiving grace. Live in the freedom of grace and renounce the erroneous belief that we get right with God by flawless compliance with the Law, which Jesus called the "yeast of the Pharisees" (Matthew 16:6,11-12).

Many of us find it easier to forgive others than to forgive ourselves. Try practicing the reverse side of the Golden Rule: "Do unto yourself as you do to others"—or the reverse of the Great Commandment: "Love yourself as you love others."

Free yourself from the illusion that you are the final judge. Our sense of unworthiness is a subtle form of arrogance, whereby we choose not to forgive the one whom God has decisively forgiven. As C. S. Lewis noted: "If God forgives us we must forgive ourselves. Otherwise it is almost like setting up ourselves as a higher tribunal than him."[7] Another put it this way: "To be pitiless or angry with ourselves and our imperfections and failures is only more of the self's . . . illusion of possible perfection."[8]

Guilt that remains after these steps have been taken may be due to woundedness inflicted by others. This may involve a wound consciously inflicted (statements like "You will never amount to anything") or unconsciously inflicted through thoughtless inattention or neglect. Emotional wounds should be addressed through healing prayer. Prayer for inner healing recognizes the difference between a sin that needs to be forgiven and a wound that needs to be healed. It may be helpful for the wounded party to participate in a liturgy of forgiveness and reconciliation that symbolically dramatizes God's forgiving grace on our behalf.

A PRAYER

LORD, when I am afflicted by false guilt, help me to remember the Cross, and to forgive myself as You, Lord, have forgiven me.

And when I am stricken by true guilt, I will pray the prayer of the psalmist, who said: "I acknowledged my sin to you and did not cover up my iniquity . . . 'I will confess my transgressions to the LORD'— and you forgave the guilt of my sin" (Psalm 32:5).

TRY IT YOURSELF

1. Try this exercise in self-examination:

Through prayerful reflection, identify an occasion when you were burdened with a significant sense of guilt, where God seemed distant and forgiveness appeared beyond reach. Feel the effects of this on your life. Was what you experienced true guilt or false guilt?

2. Describe the impact this sense of guilt had on your spiritual and emotional health.

Draw a line chart that represents the condition of your soul during that distressing leg of your journey.

As you look back in time, what persons or ministries did God providentially bring into your life to relieve your guilt?

The Barrenness of Busyness

A DEDICATED YOUNG WOMAN NAMED SUE SERVED IN A THRIVING YOUTH ministry in a suburban church. She created many attractive programs for the teenagers, and a lot of young people came to know the Lord as a result. Because of her patient dedication, many of them grew in their faith through her ministry. There was just something wonderful about Sue, and she was well-liked by the young people, their parents, and other church staff.

From the outside Sue was a model Christian and youth worker; she seemed to "have it all together."

But as ministry demands increased Sue spent less time in God's presence, nourishing her soul. As the months passed she became increasingly irritable and unhappy. Like Martha in Luke's gospel, Sue became stressed out by the compulsion to produce results. Colleagues observed that Sue became critical of others who performed at a lower level than she did. And—no surprise—her effectiveness in ministry slowly declined.

In a moment of truth one day, Sue confessed to a soul friend that she had been a performance-driven person for years. When she was a college student, her well-meaning pastor had urged her to "burn out for Jesus." Now she recognized that the pressures and stress of ministry had crippled her relationship with God. Painfully, Sue spoke of "the ministry monster that has mastered me."

Sue's experience of "hitting the wall" became a catalyst for self-examination, with her friend's support. Gradually, she changed her lifestyle. Most importantly, she learned how to relax and enjoy God's presence first and foremost . . . and in time she experienced a renewal of spiritual passion.

Today, Sue is a strong proponent of the kind of spiritual direction Jesus gave to another "high-performance" disciple long ago.

Martha's Frenetic Service

Luke 10:38-42
Traveling to Jerusalem to celebrate the Feast of Tabernacles, Jesus and His men found themselves in the village of Bethany. The tired travelers went to the home of Martha and Mary to share a meal with their friends.

Before the evening meal Jesus was reclining at the long, low table on which food was about to be served, as that was the custom of the day. Mary had been helping Martha in the kitchen, but she left the cooking and joined the men who were absorbed with Jesus and His teaching. Mary eagerly focused on Jesus, and sat down to learn at His feet—the very feet she would soon anoint with expensive perfume (see John 12:3). Devoted to God, Mary was doing what Jesus had commanded in the Sermon on the Mount: She was seeking the kingdom of God and His righteousness before all else (see Matthew 6:33).

In the kitchen, "Martha was distracted (literally, 'overburdened') by all the preparations that had to be made" (verse 40). Apparently, she was overly concerned with making everything "just right" for their honored guests. The demands of arranging the house and cooking the food pulled Martha this way and that, keeping her away from Jesus and His life-giving words. Maybe she was seeking approval by trying to get it all perfect.

It didn't take long before Martha realized she was on her own in the kitchen, with all this work to do. Her sister was no longer helping out! Instead, Mary was just sitting there at the table with Jesus.

Filled with self-pity, Martha became irritated that her sister was unwilling to help with the preparations. Martha interpreted Mary's worshipful attitude as laziness. We can hear Martha cry in frustration, "There's so much work to be done and so few hands to do it." When she could stand it no longer, she wiped her hands on a towel, made her way to Jesus, and scolded Him. "Lord," she chided, "don't you care that my sister has left me to do the work by myself? Tell her to help me!" (verse 40). It was evident that Martha was peeved at Jesus for permitting Mary simply to sit there, focused on Him.

With a sigh, Jesus tenderly said to her, "Martha, Martha . . . you are worried and upset about many things" (verse 41). Martha was a woman of faith, and we know this because elsewhere she confessed Jesus as "the Christ, the Son of God, who was to come into the world" (John 11:27). But now under stress, Martha lost it. Allowing the pressures of service to overwhelm her, she'd succumbed to the tyranny of the flesh.

Jesus patiently redirected her, saying, "Only one thing is needed. Mary has chosen what is better, and it will not be taken away from her" (verse 42). The Lord contrasted the one better thing Mary had chosen—to focus on Him and His word—to the many things (verse 41) that stressed Martha. Jesus in effect said to Martha, "What's more important? Focusing attention on Me, or anxiously striving to get your personal agenda just right?" Mary, on the other hand, received Jesus' approval, because her love for Him was more important than getting the potatoes cooked just so or the napkins properly folded. Mary got it right. She preferred to be an intimate of the Savior rather than the envy of the neighborhood. Jesus would not allow Martha to deprive Mary of her loving devotion to Him.

Jesus Ministers Spiritual Direction

FOR THOSE OF us who have the tendency to live in overdrive, draining ourselves of vitality, peace, and happiness, Jesus has spiritual direction to offer from His encounter with these sisters.

Jesus understood the unique personalities of Martha and Mary, and related to them accordingly.

Martha appears to have been a "TJ" (thinking/judging) type, and Mary an "FP" (feeling/perceiving) type. Martha by nature was more action-oriented (see John 12:2), Mary more relational and heart-centered (see John 12:3). Jesus affirmed the strength of each personality without trying to change their God-created distinctiveness.

He showed loving concern for His frustrated friend Martha.

Jesus showed unfailing love for Martha in her compulsive busyness. The Lord's compassion was seen in His tenderly repeating her name twice, "Martha, Martha," as He would do on later occasions to others: "Simon, Simon" (Luke 22:31) and "Saul, Saul" (Acts 9:4).

Jesus supported Martha by acknowledging her agitation and distress.

Jesus reflected to Martha her deep sense of helplessness and frustration. He was careful not to trivialize her irritations and anxieties; and because Martha sensed that Jesus heard her concerns and empathized with her frustrations, she listened seriously to Him.

Jesus gently corrected Martha's misplaced priorities and excessive busyness.

The Lord appreciated Martha's desire to get the arrangements just right. But He knew that her busywork distracted her heart from kingdom values. By a tender but firm rebuke Jesus brought stressed-out Martha back to her spiritual priority. He helped her see that practical demands must not crowd out communion with Him. Jesus made His point with Martha, not by condemning her but by commending Mary: "Mary has chosen what is best." Jesus practiced the principle of "positive reinforcement."

Jesus was directive in urging Martha along the path of simplicity.

Jesus' words, "Only one thing is needed," pointed Martha to the simple life focused on kingdom priorities. For Jesus, simple dinner fare (see Luke 10:8) with reverence is better than elaborate preparations with much stress. The life consumed with busyness is the fragmented life. The psalmist said,

"One thing I ask of the LORD, this is what I seek: that I may dwell in the house of the LORD all the days of my life, to gaze upon the beauty of the LORD and to seek him in his temple" (Psalm 27:4).

The Demon of Busyness

Are we really aware of what the pressure of busyness does to us?
"We're a nation of stressed-out strivers," reports *USA TODAY*.[1] Corporate downsizing, globalization, and technology (including "labor-saving" devices) pressure us from all sides. Americans are working an extra month each year compared with twenty years ago. A majority of adults suffer an hour or more per day of sleep deprivation. More than four out of five people say they have significant stress in their lives.[2] Ask a typical Christian how she's doing, and you are likely to hear, "I'm so busy. My life is crazy." There's no time to read a poem or listen to soothing music. Busyness! Pressure! Speed! So much to do, and so little time in which to do it.

Hurried busyness has invaded the church. I recently read about a church in Florida that advertises, "EXPRESS WORSHIP, 45 MINUTES, GUARANTEED!" The pastor explained, "It's an opportunity for people in our church who are running in the fast lane but still love the Lord."

Why do we drive ourselves so relentlessly? We schedule ourselves to the eyebrows to make the best impression or to prove our worth. We distort the philosopher Descartes' maxim, "I think, therefore I am," to read, "I work hard, therefore I am." Some relish busyness and speed to avoid facing up to their real selves and the haunting emptiness within.

What does all this busyness cost us?
The pace of modern life leaves us emotionally frazzled. Chuck Swindoll somewhere said, "Busyness rapes relationship. It substitutes shallow frenzy for deep friendship. It feeds the ego but stresses the inner being. It fills a calendar but fractures a family." The sign in a Christian bookstore read, "Satan doesn't need very many demons to torment Americans. He has day-timers and calendars." The busyness syndrome is a prescription for spiritual burnout. Like Martha, we can become frazzled while doing God's work.

More seriously, excessive busyness creates a disconnect with God. The busyness syndrome quenches the Spirit and renders God a haunting stranger. The hurried and harried soul discovers that God's gracious visitations become all too rare. Thomas Merton said, "Unnatural, frantic, anxious work done under pressure of . . . inordinate passion cannot properly be dedicated to God, because God never wills such work."[3]

Jesus' life was never controlled by the clock or by circumstances. We never find Jesus rushing to a celebration at Cana or hurrying to meet a Samaritan woman at Sychar. His manner was always measured and collected. Jesus served with a calmness and composure rooted in communion with the Father.

How can we shed the yoke of busyness and follow the better way chosen by Mary?

We can realize that God created us as human beings, not human doings. Who we are is not defined by what we do. Significance derives from our creation as image of God and our identity in Christ. We can never perform sufficiently to earn God's favor; we simply receive and enjoy what He freely gives. The outflow of our defining relationship with God will be reasonable service—not flawless performance—according to God's will. Evelyn Underhill has said, "We mostly spend [our] lives conjugating 3 verbs: to *want*, to *have*, and to *do*."[4] Surely our greatest need is simply to *be*, like Mary dwelling in the presence of God.

We can prayerfully establish priorities and evaluate our commitments. Like Martha, we need to get our priorities straight and choose the "better" way—pursuit of Christ. Life is too short to fulfill all the obligations thrust upon us. If we fail to cultivate a nourishing relationship with the Lord, the "better" will be crowded out by a thousand "necessities." Fellowship with Jesus must not be bartered away by the tyranny of the urgent.

We can intentionally create margins in our life. We need to be countercultural in cultivating a milieu for meeting God: space, stillness, and solitude. Creatively carve out Sabbath spaces in your daily routine. Faithfully keep the weekly Sabbath. Resting from six days of work creates the environment in which we can rest in God. Only as we create intentional space for God will He show up in our experience.

We can explore the grace of contemplation. A pastor friend related, "Evangelicals run in overdrive from morning till night with little time for pious reflection." To cultivate relationship with God we must slow down, sit at Jesus' feet, and focus the eye of the heart on Him. We must listen to the still, small voice of God and respond obediently. We must pray, both with words and without words. We must receive in order that we may be equipped to give.

A. W. Tozer put it this way: Petitionary prayer, Bible study, and Christian service "are all good and should be engaged in by every Christian. But at the bottom of all these things, giving meaning to them will be the inward habit of beholding God . . . When the habit of inwardly gazing Godward becomes fixed within us, we shall be ushered onto a new level of spiritual life more in keeping with the promises of God and the mood of the New Testament."[5]

We can live a balanced life of contemplation and action. There's a time for reflection and worship and a time for service and action. Pious reflection informs and empowers action. Action in turn deepens reflection on kingdom priorities. The God-honoring life involves both the vertical relation of devotion to God (Mary) and the horizontal relation of service to the neighbor (the best of Martha). God planned the pattern of contemplation and action, for Jesus confirmed the proper answer: "'Love the Lord your God . . .' and 'Love your neighbor as yourself'" (Luke 10:27).

A Prayer

Lord, You know how easily I substitute soul-depleting activity for the blessing of unencumbered time in Your presence. Help me to imitate Mary, whose greatest passion was to know and worship You.

Try It Yourself

1. Take stock of your life.

It has been said that most middle-class Americans tend to worship their work, to work at their play, and to play at their worship.

Keep track of your personal schedule for a week or two. How many hours a week do you work at your job or profession?

How many hours a day or week do you spend with God in quietness, prayer, and meditation?

Do you observe the weekly Sabbath as a day of worship, rest, and personal renewal?

2. Identify a friend with whom you can be mutually accountable to create margins in your life and schedule quality time with God.

Self-Sufficient in Wealth

BRAD GRADUATED FROM A CHRISTIAN COLLEGE WITH A DEGREE IN finance. At the outset of his career his intention was to serve the Lord in the business world.

He landed his first job with a construction company. Later he founded his own real-estate development firm and bought up large parcels of residential and commercial property. Later he planned and developed the largest business and industrial park in the city. Prosperous business ventures allowed him to purchase a country home and take foreign vacations.

All the while, Brad, his wife, Carla, and their children participated in the activities of a large suburban church. But Brad kept himself apart from any meaningful fellowship. After a number of years in the business world, Brad confided to an associate that his goal was "to make a pile of money."

Reviewing his assets, Brad's accountant told him that he was worth ten million dollars. When asked what his next goal was, Brad shrugged and replied, "*Fifty* million."

One day when he returned home late from work Brad was confronted by Carla. Through tears she said, "I don't love you anymore. You're married to your financial empire. It's become your master. I can't stay in this loveless marriage."

Within days, Carla packed up her things, left with the children, and filed for divorce. Brad's response was to devote himself even more energetically to his business ventures. Sadly, eighteen months later, Brad was charged with embezzling funds from private investors in a large real-estate scheme. Before his court appearance, however, Brad fled the country for a foreign location in order to escape prosecution.

Many are the men and women in our culture who become self-sufficient by trusting in their money or possessions. To these people, Jesus has much to say by way of spiritual direction.

The Rich Young Ruler

Mark 10:17-22; Matthew 19:16-22; Luke 18:18-23

One day, a young Jewish civil official ran up to Jesus and fell on his knees. The man was intelligent, morally upright . . . and rich. It seemed he'd realized that there was more to life than position and possessions when he asked Jesus, "What good thing must I do to get eternal life?" (Matthew 19:16). Perhaps he thought Jesus was going to direct him to do some notable work, or to give some benevolent donation—something clear and simple that would gain him a ticket to heaven without disturbing his lavish lifestyle. Jesus' response was an attempt to lift the young man's vision heavenward: "Why do you ask me about what is good? . . . There is only One who is good. If you want to enter life, obey the commandments" (Matthew 19:17).

"Which ones?" the young man asked.

In reply, Jesus quoted from the second table of the Law—the one that clearly identifies obligations to one's neighbor: "Do not murder, do not commit adultery, do not steal, do not give false testimony, honor your father and mother, and 'love your neighbor as yourself'" (Matthew 19:18-19). (Conduct toward others is, of course, a barometer of the spiritual condition of one's heart.)

The young man responded that he scored well in dealings with his fellow man. Since his *bar-mitzvah*, when according to Judaism he became morally accountable, he had lived an upright life. He had not killed, stolen, or been sexually immoral. "What do I still lack?" the man asked. The rich ruler's question revealed his ignorance of the spirit of God's Law as well as a hint of false piety and pride.

Mark records that "Jesus looked at him and loved him" (Mark 10:21), much as a parent's heart goes out in compassion to a child who is struggling to find his way. And then Jesus addressed the young man's core issue head-on: "One thing you lack . . . Go, sell everything you have and give to the poor, and you will have treasure in heaven. Then come, follow me" (Mark 10:21). Jesus implied that it is impossible to add the icing of eternal life to the cake of a self-indulgent lifestyle. This rich young man must exchange earthly riches for heavenly treasures and follow Jesus as His loyal disciple.

Stunned silence filled the moment as the rich man reasoned, "'Sell everything'? How can I pay such a price?"

The story ends tragically: "When he heard this, he became very sad, because he was a man of great wealth" (Luke 18:23). Jesus was testing the man in his pocketbook, and he failed the exam. He treasured his possessions more than the "good teacher" whose counsel he sought. He could live without God, but not without his possessions.

The young man went away brokenhearted. He forfeited the blessing offered in Mary's song of exultation: "He has filled the hungry with good things" (Luke 1:53a); and he realized the desolation spoken of in Mary's next breath: "[He] has sent the rich away empty" (verse 53b).

Jesus Ministers Spiritual Direction

Jesus' encounter with the wealthy young official provides insights into our Lord's practice of spiritual guidance with someone whose earthly ties are keeping him from God.

Jesus exercised discernment and wisdom as He penetrated the rich man's inner world.

The Lord read the young ruler's heart and identified his ruling passion: wealth and possessions. Discerning that the man was an intellectual type, which presents its own particular difficulties, Jesus brought the man down to issues of the heart. All three Synoptic Gospels place the story of the rich young ruler after Jesus' teaching about the necessity of becoming like little children in simplicity and trust.

Jesus showed great compassion for the man in his search for life's meaning.

By honestly admitting that something important was missing in his life, the rich man became vulnerable. Jesus didn't exploit his vulnerability, but enveloped him with self-giving love. Such an expression of love should have given the rich man the confidence to trust Jesus.

Jesus was nondirective in the counterquestion He posed to the man.

The Lord did not answer the ruler's question directly, but posed His own — "Why do you ask me about what is good?" — to invite the official to begin a journey of self-discovery. It probed his motives, illumined the state of his soul, and communicated the vision of the grander world he sought, but did not fully understand.

Jesus knew the Scriptures and applied them to the specific needs of the rich man's heart.

Citing God's commandments from memory, Jesus pointed out the official's failure to measure up to God's holy standard. As the apostle Paul later put it, "Through the law we become conscious of sin" (Romans 3:20).

Jesus was directive in ministering spiritual guidance.

Jesus' ministry of spiritual guidance to the rich ruler was directive, involving several specific commands: "*go . . . sell . . . give . . . come . . . follow.*" The Lord urged the rich man to take the necessary steps to lay hold of eternal life. He must choose to embrace a new master.

Jesus faced resistance in spiritual direction.
Although sincere in his search for truth, the rich man refused to surrender his god of wealth and follow Jesus. Presented with the opportunity to embrace the gold that will never perish, the man chose cheap, earthly imitations. The Lord allowed the rich man freedom to reject the truth. Sadly, some of our own efforts at spiritual direction do not turn out as positively as we desire.

The Handicap of Riches

THE RICH RULER who asked Jesus about the path to heaven had great possessions, but did not realize that his possessions had *him*. He is a model of modern man, who worships the constellated deity of possessions, power, and prestige.

Jesus never taught that material possessions are sinful in themselves. Every bounty comes from the beneficent hand of the Creator (see Psalm 24:1). Abraham (see Genesis 24:35), Job (see Job 1:3), and Solomon (see 1 Kings 3:13; 10:23) were blessed with abundant material possessions. In the Old Testament, wealth was a sign of God's blessing and favor (see Job 42:10; 1 Chronicles 29:12). The kind of dualism that tells us we must renounce material possessions in order to be spiritual or pleasing to God is unbiblical.

Nonetheless, material possessions can never satisfy the undying human soul sculpted in the divine image. Material goods scintillate the senses for a while, but soon lose their glow. A wealthy man was asked how much it would take to make him really happy. His reply: "Just a little more." As the Teacher put it millennia ago, "Those who love money will never have enough. How absurd to think that wealth brings true happiness!" (Ecclesiastes 5:10, NLT). So Jesus warned against the "deceitfulness of wealth" (Matthew 13:22).

Although wealth is not intrinsically sinful, it does expose us to many subtle snares. Paul wrote, "People who long to be rich fall into temptation and are trapped by many foolish and harmful desires that plunge them into ruin and destruction" (1 Timothy 6:9, NLT). Wealth and possessions encourage self-trust rather than God-trust. That's why Jesus said, "It is easier for a camel to go through the eye of a needle than for a rich man to enter the kingdom of God" (Mark 10:25). C. S. Lewis wrote, "If everything seems to come simply by signing cheques, you may forget that you are at every moment totally dependent on God."[1]

The passion for riches breeds a host of daughter vices. Love of wealth chokes off spiritual life (see Matthew 13:22); and as Augustine remarked, "The love of worldly possessions is a sort of birdlime, which entangles the soul and prevents it flying to God."[2] The quest for riches fosters anxiety (see

Matthew 6:25-34), breeds greed (see Romans 1:29; Ephesians 5:3), spawns injustice (see James 5:4-6), and leads to crimes of theft (see Joshua 7:21) and murder (see 1 Kings 21). Wealth also drains us of time. When we own something—a fancy boat or a big house —it owns some of our time in return.

We must avoid the love of money, which corrupts the soul. Marlon Brando once said, "The only reason I'm in Hollywood is that I don't have the moral courage to say no to the money." The bottom line is that Jesus told us that only one Master can rule us: Himself (see Matthew 23:8). Unfortunately, we do not take Him at His word. We want to be Donald Trump and Billy Graham all rolled into one.

How does a Christian move from being possessed by one's possessions to delight in God and generosity to others? Consider the following principles.

Acknowledge that God alone is your highest good.

Not earthly possessions, but only God alone can satisfy the human soul (see Psalm 81:16; 145:16). Let your heart's passion be that of the psalmist, who declared, "Whom have I in heaven but you? And earth has nothing I desire besides you" (Psalm 73:25). Find your joy and consolation in God rather than in the tinseled attractions of this world. If you are a Christian, focus on the spiritual riches you have in Christ (see 2 Corinthians 8:9). Possessing Him, you possess everything. Augustine put it this way: "Listen to me, you who are poor: what is lacking to you if you have God? Listen to me, you who are rich: what do you possess if you do not have God?"[3]

Through prayer and fasting, discern how worldly possessions may have a grip on your life.

The first step to finding our way out of a self-made prison is to identify the master that holds us in bondage. Honestly ask yourself some hard questions: What material things might be weighing my soul down? How might my expenditures be demeaning to, or exploitative of, others? Often prayers are not answered because "you ask with wrong motives, that you may spend what you get on your pleasures" (James 4:3).

Loosen your grip on material things by enlarging love for Christ.

An inverse relationship exists between our longing for things and our love for Christ (see John 3:30). As Augustine put it, "Souls rise more to spiritual things the more they die to fleshly things."[4] Displace what is lowly with an infinitely higher attraction. Drive a spike through the master of possessions by intensifying fascination with Jesus. "Keep your lives free from the love of money and be content with what you have" (Hebrews 13:5).

Surrender your resources to God.

Because all that we possess are gifts from God, we are but stewards of His bounty. Capture the vision for the compassionate use of resources on loan to us. Pray for the grace of a "cheerful giver" (see 2 Corinthians 9:6-7). Heed Wesley's instruction to Christians of his day: "Make all you can; save all you can; give all you can"[5]; and follow Jesus' instruction: "Do not store up for yourselves treasures on earth, where moth and rust destroy, and where thieves break in and steal. But store up for yourselves treasures in heaven, where moth and rust do not destroy, and where thieves do not break in and steal" (Matthew 6:19-20).

Remember that disciples through the ages joyfully gave up everything to follow Jesus.

Armed with the vision of an unshakable world to come, disciples in every century left homes, careers, and earthly goods to follow Jesus. The surrender of everything below is insignificant compared to the glory that lies above. Those willing to follow know the truth of Augustine's words: "How great and wonderful is the joy of Christian generosity we obtain when, in obedience to the gospel of Christ, we cheerfully sacrifice what that rich man grieved over and refused to give up."[6]

A PRAYER

LORD, my natural human inclination is to set my heart on, and find my security in, material things. Grant me the grace to be possessed, not by my possessions, but by You, the Lover of my soul.

TRY IT YOURSELF

1. Try gaining the eternal perspective.

Reflect on the following statement by Athanasius (d. 373), a great leader of the early church:

> When we die we will leave [temporal riches] behind to those we do not want to have them. Why then wouldn't we give them up for righteousness' sake in order to inherit a kingdom? Don't let the desire to possess things take hold of you. For what do we gain by acquiring things we cannot take with us? Why not get the things we can take with us instead—namely wisdom, justice, self-control, courage, understanding, love, kindness to the poor, faith in Christ, freedom from wrath, and hospitality? If we possess these things, they will prepare a welcome for us in the land of the humble.[7]

2. **Search your heart to determine if you have allowed temporal things to deflect your heart from God.**
What kind of spiritual disciplines or activities would allow you to loosen your grip on material possessions and grasp more firmly kingdom priorities?

3. **Make a pact with your spouse or a close friend for mutual accountability in the matter of finances and material possessions.**

Exploiter of Others

THE OWNER OF A SLATE QUARRY IN A WESTERN STATE EMPLOYED LEGAL immigrant workers to mine and cut slate slabs. The Mexican workers, most of whom didn't speak English, were required to labor under a hot summer sun from early morning to late evening, then return home to living conditions that were appalling.

Most workers were housed in broken-down trailers with plastic tarps over the roofs to keep out the rain. Often an entire family was sheltered in a single, small space. Kitchen facilities were primitive and unclean. Bathing and toilet facilities were communal and highly unsanitary—no more than an outhouse minus a door. Medical care for the workers and their families was virtually nonexistent. The workers' living conditions later would be condemned by the state Health Department.

As the summer went on the quarry owner, citing a weak economy, withheld several weeks of the workers' wages. Soon thereafter their paychecks ceased, even though the slate they quarried continued to be sold and shipped to customers. Through an interpreter the immigrant workers protested their living conditions and the withholding of their wages. The quarry owner told them to quit complaining or he'd take away their permits and have them all deported.

Powerless, in a bad predicament, the workers stopped their complaints, fearing deportation and the loss of future wages to support their families.

Some people, like this employer, are masters of exploitation. We may not be so blatant and callous, but each of us has the tendency to use other people in some way for our own ends. We can all benefit from a clear-eyed look at the way Jesus ministered soul care to someone who exploited others.

Zacchaeus at Jericho

Luke 19:1-10
The story of Jesus' meeting with Zacchaeus is one of the best-known in Scripture. Jesus entered Jericho followed by a crowd of onlookers as He headed for the final showdown in Jerusalem. With its spring-fed water supply, palm-lined streets, and fragrant flowers, Jericho was a little paradise.

The Roman politician and soldier Marc Antony had given Jericho to the Egyptian queen Cleopatra as a sign of his affection. In Jesus' day, the palace of Herod the Great was located there.

To the locals, Jericho was a hated place because it was a center for collecting tariffs on goods entering from the East. Under normal circumstances, Jesus would have passed through Jericho. But He lingered, knowing there was important ministry to do. Enter Zacchaeus, a Jew who served the Romans as a chief tax collector.

Imperial Rome levied heavy taxes on the nations they subjugated. The chief tax collector contracted to pay the Roman authorities a fixed sum of money; he then hired assistants to collect taxes and kept the rest of the revenue for himself. Rank-and-file Jews resented the fact that one of their own padded his pocket and that their taxes supported an idol-worshipping regime. Zacchaeus, a Jew, was the taxman for the Romans. Wealthy, hard, he was seen as an extortionist and a traitor, the most despised man in town.

Driven by curiosity and an inner restlessness, Zacchaeus wanted to see Jesus as He passed through town. But a large crowd had gathered to catch sight of the man they thought might deliver Israel from Roman oppression. Zacchaeus was barely five feet tall, so he couldn't see the Rabbi for the crowd. He ran ahead and climbed a sycamore tree, with its broad branches and shady leaves.

When Jesus reached the place where Zacchaeus perched, He looked up and said, "Zacchaeus, come down immediately. I must stay at your house today" (verse 5). The Greek word for must, *dei*, conveys the idea of divine necessity. "Today" (used eleven times in Luke) signifies the moment of salvation. Shocked, Zacchaeus slid down the tree and welcomed Jesus and His disciples into his home.

We can imagine that the crowd snickered over Jesus saddling up with this swindler and turncoat. Jesus would become defiled eating in a publican's house. It was a bad connection. Luke compressed the story, but we can believe that Jesus and Zacchaeus had dinner together and engaged in serious conversation. I suspect that Jesus invited Zacchaeus to tell his story, and He probably asked him questions such as, "How have you treated the common people?" and "How did you get so wealthy?" Jesus listened attentively to his story and to his deepest aspirations. His genuine compassion for Zacchaeus must have softened the publican's heart in faith-filled surrender.

In the presence of the Lord, Zacchaeus freely admitted that he had cheated his fellow countrymen. He offered to make full restitution and more. According to Roman law, he would repay those he defrauded fourfold. And he would give half of his wealth to the poor. Zacchaeus found healing and freedom in making reparation for the wrongs inflicted. The publican who met Jesus as a cheat and extorter left that meeting a radically changed man. But . . .

The crowd wanted Zacchaeus punished. Jesus would not buy into their desire for retribution. Instead He celebrated the publican's spiritual rebirth, saying, "Today salvation has come to this house, because this man, too, is a son of Abraham" (verse 9). Zacchaeus became a follower of Jesus; and according to the church father Clement of Alexandria (d. 215), he was ordained bishop of Caesarea.

Through generosity of spirit, an exploiter of men was transformed into a generous son of God.

Jesus Ministers Spiritual Direction

JESUS' INTERACTION WITH the chief tax collector offers insights into the Lord's ministry of spiritual guidance for even those who are despised for good reason and thus, friends of no one.

Jesus discerned the Father's call to minister grace to the despised publican.
Jesus sensed that He had a divine appointment with that lost son of Abraham, the soil of whose heart was prepared by the Holy Spirit. He interrupted His journey to do what His Father wanted Him to do. Jesus allowed neither the man's political views nor exploitative lifestyle to get in the way of ministry to him.

Jesus sought out the spiritually hungry publican.
Jesus took the initiative to engage Zacchaeus. He ordered the official to come down from the shelter of the tree and boldly invited Himself to Zacchaeus' house (see verse 5). There, He opened Zacchaeus' eyes to spiritual reality.

From this we see that, while Zacchaeus was searching for a better way, Jesus was searching for Zacchaeus—even before the man could articulate his own need. All Zacchaeus needed to do was stop running from God. Yahweh said, "I revealed myself to those who did not ask for me; I was found by those who did not seek me" (Isaiah 65:1).

Jesus looked behind Zacchaeus' exploitative lifestyle and loved and accepted him as a valued person corrupted by his own false choices.
Jesus loved the sinful publican and discerned the needs of his heart, his very thoughts, as He had for so many others before (see Luke 5:22; 6:8; 9:47). The Lord looked beyond the Roman agent's evil deeds to envision what he might become by grace.

Jesus' ministry to Zacchaeus was both directive and nondirective.
On the main road through Jericho, Jesus told Zacchaeus exactly what he must do: he must come down from the tree and join Him at the table. When Jesus invited Himself to Zacchaeus' house He said, in effect, "God is willing to forgive you." Jesus also gave Zacchaeus space for self-discovery as the two dialogued together in his home.

Jesus led Zacchaeus to a repentance that resulted in generous reparations.
Ordinary Jews who had been exploited by Zacchaeus thought the traitor to be beyond repair. But Jesus came to seek out and save the worst of lost sinners (see verse 10). The Lord empowered Zacchaeus to turn from his sin to God and to make full restitution to those he had defrauded. The camel, indeed, passed through the eye of a needle! (See Luke 18:25.)

The Burden of Oppression

THE STORY OF Zacchaeus illustrates man's inhumanity to his fellowman and Jesus' response to the self-serving exploiter. Motivated by greed, the publican bled his fellow citizens of their hard-earned money.

Exploitation and oppression can occur in the family, the workplace, society, and among nations. In the family, a husband may put his wife down and be insensitive to her needs under the guise of male—or even worse, spiritual—leadership. At the national level, Native Americans were driven from productive land into remote and barren reservations.

Whatever form it takes, exploitation is a violation of God-given human dignity. Exploitative practices deprive people of the necessities of life and assail their worth. Conservative Christians often overlook political and economic injustice, choosing to focus on more "spiritual" concerns. But in the real world, nothing is purely "spiritual." All choices have material and social consequences—and all have a spiritual aspect.

God's response to sin and evil is the life, death, and resurrection of His Son. The context of God's work of salvation, however, is the social matrix of family, community, nation, and the world of nations. These must be governed by principles of truth, justice, and compassion.

Jesus' ministry to Zacchaeus addressed both his spiritual need and his social behavior. The Lord birthed supernatural life into Zacchaeus' soul; but he was also deeply concerned with the consequences of the publican's unjust actions. Christians must be passionate about the salvation of souls *and* social righteousness. God says, "Woe to those who . . . deprive the poor of their rights and withhold justice from the oppressed of my people, making widows their prey and robbing the fatherless" (Isaiah 10:1-2).

Consider the following guidelines, which suggest ways to minister to a person like Zacchaeus, trapped in a pattern of exploitative behavior.

We can lead the person to recognize the error of his ways.

Guide the wayward person to recognize his sinful behavior pattern and its harmful consequences to others. Repentance requires a fundamental change of mind in the sinner. "Let the wicked forsake his way and the evil man his thoughts. Let him turn to the LORD, and he will have mercy on him" (Isaiah 55:7).

We can help the oppressing person to feel remorse for her actions.

There must be a grieving that comes from a heart distressed by one's hurtful actions. Repentance requires mourning for sin at the level of feeling. "Then you will remember your evil ways and wicked deeds, and you will loathe yourselves for your sins and detestable practices" (Ezekiel 36:31). According to Paul, "Godly sorrow brings repentance that leads to salvation and leaves no regret" (2 Corinthians 7:10).

We can guide the erring person to the Lord in genuine repentance.

There must be a deliberate turning from unjust behavior to God in faith. Repentance requires a fundamental change of heart. Chastened by the Lord, Ephraim confessed, "After I strayed, I repented; after I came to understand, I beat my breast. I was ashamed and humiliated because I bore the disgrace of my youth" (Jeremiah 31:19). We must also understand that heartfelt repentance is a work of God's grace (see Acts 5:31; 2 Timothy 2:25).

We can encourage the wayward to make full restitution to those they have exploited.

Wrongs inflicted need to be made right by restoration of property, return of money, or service as compensation for damage done. The Law spelled out what steps had to be taken to set things right within Israel (see Exodus 22:1-14; Leviticus 6:1-5; Numbers 5:5-7); and Paul preached that sinners "should repent and turn to God and prove their repentance by their deeds" (Acts 26:20). The church father Chrysostom (d. 407) wrote, "Don't give thanks only with your words, but through your works and actions."[1]

A PRAYER

LORD, I am prone to use other people in a multitude of ways for my own aggrandizement. As Your disciple, empower me to love others and deal justly with them as images of God so they might be attracted to You, the God I follow and serve.

TRY IT YOURSELF

1. Try this exercise in *Lectio Divina*.

Lectio involves reflectively reading a text of Scripture, pausing to meditate on a significant word or phrase, praying that word back to the Father, then listening attentively to the Spirit's voice.

Do a lectio on the following Scripture:

> For our offenses are many in your sight,
> and our sins testify against us.
> Our offenses are ever with us,
> and we acknowledge our iniquities:
> rebellion and treachery against the LORD,
> turning our backs on our God,
> fomenting oppression and revolt,
> uttering lies our hearts have conceived.
> So justice is driven back,
> and righteousness stands at a distance;
> truth has stumbled in the streets,
> honesty cannot enter. (Isaiah 59:12-15)

Are you aware of any sin of injustice or oppression you have committed against another?

How has the fault you identified confounded truth and justice?

2. Take time for extended reflection.

Reflect on how this sin has impacted your relationship with God. Confess the wrongdoing now to the Lord.

What actions are needed to make restitution for this fault?

Betrayal of Trust

JULIAN (331-363), NEPHEW OF CONSTANTINE THE GREAT, THE FIRST Christian emperor, lived during the declining years of the Roman Empire. Julian was privately educated in the Bible and the Greek and Roman classics by the best tutors. He was baptized as a Christian and participated in the life and worship of the church. He personally knew many prominent Christian leaders and theologians of his day. At age 23, Julian became co-regent with his cousin, Constantius II. But the young man who showed so much faith and promise was to surprise everyone.

Sent to Gaul to defend the Empire from the West, Julian won battle after battle against the pagans. His cousin became jealous of the young man's military prowess and ordered most of his forces to return to Rome. Julian's men refused, and proudly proclaimed him emperor. Constantius died shortly thereafter, leaving Julian the sole head of the Roman Empire.

Modeling his reign after Marcus Aurelius, Julian at first instituted positive reforms. He eliminated corruption, reduced taxes, and promoted religious toleration. But it wasn't long before Julian took off his mask and openly identified himself with Greco-Roman paganism. Julian rebuilt pagan temples, restored worship of the classical gods and goddesses, and forbade Christians from holding public office. He replaced the cross imprinted on military equipment with pagan symbols. He also published the antiChristian work, *Against the Galileans*. On the battlefield, Julian's soldiers crushed cities that claimed the name of Christ. In one battle, Julian was struck by a spear and died, reigning as Roman emperor for only two years. He would have disappeared into relative obscurity, except that historians gave him the title, "Julian the Apostate."

Julian is an example of extreme betrayal. So is the next man we're about to meet. Few people we meet will have betrayed Christ, or the Christian community, so openly and completely as these two. Yet we can learn great lessons in spiritual direction by considering how Jesus dealt with His own betrayer.

Judas' Betrayal

John 13:18-30; Matthew 26:20-25

On a Thursday evening near the end of His earthly ministry, Jesus entered the Upper Room to celebrate His last Passover meal with the twelve disciples. This final gathering of Jesus and His friends was an emotional time for Him (see Luke 22:15-16). Ahead loomed the shadow of the Cross.

Three years earlier, Jesus had chosen Judas as His disciple (see Luke 6:16), undoubtedly because He saw much potential in the man. Given his financial and administrative skills, Judas was entrusted with the treasury of the Twelve. Unfortunately, he periodically stole money from the common purse for his own use (see John 12:6). Later, when Mary anointed Jesus' feet at Bethany with expensive perfume, Judas objected. He wanted the ointment sold for money that he could use himself.

After supper, Jesus compassionately washed the disciples' feet. Then He said, "He who shares my bread has lifted up his heel against me" (John 13:18). The sharing of bread together was an act of friendship and intimacy. "Raising your heel" referred to an act of contempt. On this occasion of friendship and love, Judas had only contempt for the Master he followed for three years. Like a wild horse, he was prepared to kick and trample the One who led him. Aware of what was happening, Jesus said, "I am telling you now before it happens" (John 13:19). As they gathered around the table for the meal, "Jesus was troubled in spirit" (verse 21). Like a storm at sea, the Lord's spirit was distressed that one of His close friends—a "devil" (John 6:70-71)—would betray Him. Shocked and speechless, the disciples looked at each other, wondering who the betrayer might be. They knew their own shortcomings and failures . . . but outright betrayal? The silence was stunning.

One by one the disciples asked, "Surely not I, Lord" (Matthew 26:22). Somberly Jesus added, "The Son of Man will go just as it is written about him. But woe to that man who betrays the Son of Man! It would be better for him if he had not been born" (Matthew 26:24). Peter urged John, who reclined next to Jesus, to ask the Lord to identify the betrayer. John leaned back and whispered, "Lord, who is it?" (John 13:25). With hushed voice, Jesus indicated how the traitor would be known: "It is the one to whom I will give this piece of bread when I have dipped it in the dish" (verse 26). In Eastern cultures, a host dipped a piece of bread in broth and placed it in the mouth of the guest as an offer of friendship.

Not wanting to be conspicuous by remaining silent, Judas said, "Surely not I, Rabbi?" (Matthew 26:25). Jesus placed the bread in Judas' mouth—giving him one final opportunity to repent of his treacherous deed. John added, "As soon as Judas took the bread, Satan entered into him" (verse 27). Satan had been toying with Judas for more than a year. Now in the Upper Room the evil one took possession of the traitor, and the keeper of the treasury became a pawn of the power of darkness. Discerning that Judas' condition was beyond repair, Jesus bluntly said, "What you are about to do, do quickly" (verse 27).

Immediately after taking the bread, Judas left the room with no sense of remorse. John noted, "It was night" (verse 30). Having deliberately turned his back on Jesus—the "light of the world" (John 8:12; 9:5)—Judas became engulfed in moral and spiritual darkness. Earlier Jesus warned, "Walk while you have the light, before darkness overtakes you. The man who walks in the dark does not know where he is going" (John 12:35). Augustine said of Judas, "The man who went out into the night became night himself."[1]

Judas brought his apostasy to fruition that same night. After Jesus' struggle in Gethsemane, Judas greeted the Lord with fervent kisses, then delivered Him over to the temple police for thirty silver coins (see John 18:1-9). Later, consumed with self-hatred and despair, Judas completed his cowardly course by hanging himself (see Matthew 27:3-5; Acts 1:18). Luke later stated that Judas left the circle of disciples "to go where he belongs" (Acts 1:25). Dante, in his *Vision of Hell*, placed Judas in the deepest chamber of the damned, along with Satan himself.

Jesus Ministers Spiritual Direction

JESUS' INTERACTION WITH Judas offers insight into His ministry of spiritual guidance with a companion turned traitor.

Jesus risked loving Judas, despite the possibility of being betrayed.
Jesus knew that Judas would betray Him; yet right up to the end Jesus showed His love for Judas. Moments before Judas's betrayal, Jesus washed his feet and, in a final sign of friendship, offered him a piece of bread dipped in broth.

Jesus discerned the condition of Judas' soul.
When mentoring His disciples, Jesus observed that Judas was not growing in trust and love like the others. At Bethany, where Mary anointed Jesus with fine ointment, the Lord perceived that Judas was driven by greed (see John 12:6-8). Jesus sensed in His spirit that Judas opposed His purposes and that when conditions were right he would betray Him (see John 13:2,18,21). The Lord sensed that Satan had entered Judas to accomplish his evil work (see John 6:70-71; 13:27).

Jesus was distressed in spirit by the treacherous course Judas chose.
In the Upper Room "Jesus was troubled in spirit" (John 13:21), or He
"became visibly upset" (MSG). The Lord experienced in His soul the agony of
a sacred trust betrayed. Thus He is able to empathize with persons who have
been betrayed through events such as divorce or a crooked business deal.

Jesus confronted Judas with his destructive course of action.
By saying, "I tell you the truth, one of you is going to betray me" (John
13:21), Jesus confronted His treacherous disciple with the truth. By saying
this, the Lord provided the deceitful Judas with an opportunity to examine
his motives. Jesus didn't allow the traitor to persist in deceiving himself or
others. Confronting a companion is never easy or comfortable, but Jesus
accomplished it with integrity.

**Jesus extended to the betrayer repeated opportunities to abandon his
betrayal and start over.**
The Lord's announcement of betrayal provided opportunity for Judas to
repent and rebuild the relationship. Jesus' act of offering bread as a sign of
friendship was a further invitation for Judas to turn aside of his evil deed.
When Judas resolved to betray his Master, Jesus didn't deter him from his
destructive course. The Lord honored Judas' freedom, rather than force
him into a relationship he didn't desire.

Breach of Trust

JUDAS' BETRAYAL OF trust was born out of greed for political and material gain. He joined the band of disciples believing Jesus would over-
throw Rome and proclaim Himself king. Opportunistic to the core,
Judas likely hoped to become Chancellor of the Exchequer in Jesus'
earthly kingdom.

When Judas came to understand that Jesus' kingdom was spiritual and
heavenly, he felt cheated. He became bitter and hateful toward the Lord.
The straw that broke the camel's back may have been Jesus' failure on Palm
Sunday to capitalize on the crowd's acclamation of Him as the "King of the
Jews." Convinced that the apostolic ship was sinking, Judas decided to "cut
bait" and run with whatever he could get for himself. Feeling that he had
been suckered, Judas determined to break trust and exact revenge.

The cornerstone of any relationship, trust involves loyalty, integrity,
and honesty. The trusted partner says, "I will be there to support and protect you to the end." Where trust is maintained, respect, safety, and closeness prevail. Well it is said, "Trust is the glue that binds us to one another."[2]

But trust is fragile, and can easily be broken. An unconscious breach of trust occurs, for example, when a person carelessly divulges confidential information about a friend to a third party. Deliberate betrayal of trust occurs as a calculated retaliation inflicted by a person who feels wronged and therefore "justified" in breaking covenant. Judas illustrates the deliberate betrayal of trust.

Early on, Judas was as confused and carnal as the other disciples. "But," as James Stalker put it, "there was a canker at the root of his character, which gradually absorbed all that was excellent in him, and became a tyrannical passion. It was the love of money." As time progressed, the other disciples "became ever more spiritual, he ever more worldly."[3]

The story of Judas offers a serious warning, for each of us has a part of Judas lurking in our hearts. How can we avoid betraying sacred trust with the Lord?

We can remind ourselves that as Christians we have entered into a sacred covenant with Christ.

The New Covenant is a two-sided agreement with promises to be kept. God faithfully keeps His promises to love, provide, and protect His own to the end. His promises are as good as gold. But believers must resolve to keep their side of the covenant, as well. We must uphold our end of the bargain by proving faithful to our commitment to God.

Think of the consequences of covenant keeping and covenant breaking. Peter stumbled, but repented. He went on to become a great leader and saint and received a heavenly reward. Judas betrayed trust, and refused to repent. Overcome with remorse, he took his own life and wound up in hell.

We can enter into an effective accountability relationship with at least one other disciple.

Find an accountability partner, and be transparent and truthful with him (or her). Growth in trust requires a friend who will model that virtue, point out pitfalls, and hold your feet to the fire. In covenant relationship with your spiritual partner, you will learn the goodness of trust and the evil of distrust. You will overcome the unhealthy need to seek self-gratification by inflicting revenge on others.

We can prayerfully discern the deepest motives of our hearts.

By prayerful self-examination, identify those impulses of the flesh that fuel betrayal of trust: selfishness, jealousy, greed, bitterness, and anger. Share these impulses with your accountability partner, and bring them before the Lord with earnest prayer for their removal.

We can continuously kindle our love relationship with the Lord.

We are unlikely to betray a person we truly love. *Agape* love sturdily bears hardships, disappointments, and wrongs inflicted upon us. The apostle Paul wrote:

Love cares more for others than for self.
Love doesn't want what it doesn't have. . . .
Isn't always "me first,"
Doesn't fly off the handle,
Doesn't keep score of the sins of others . . .
Trusts God always,
Always looks for the best,
Never looks back,
But keeps going to the end. (1 Corinthians 13:4-7, MSG)

A PRAYER

LORD, You have wedded me as a believer to Yourself in an everlasting covenant of love and faithfulness. Amidst life's trials, instill in me the passionate desire to be loyal and true to You until that great day when I'm ushered into Your glorious presence.

TRY IT YOURSELF

1. Meditate on a psalm of betrayal.

Psalm 55 rehearses David's response to the rebellion of his son Absalom and the betrayal of his trusted counselor, Ahithophel (see 2 Samuel 15-17). Absalom plotted to usurp the throne from David, and Ahithophel switched sides to serve as Absalom's counselor. When Absalom rejected Ahithophel's advice, the betrayer committed suicide, like Judas.

Prayerfully meditate on Psalm 55 and ask yourself the following questions:

Verses 2-5: How did David feel at the betrayal of the one he described as "my companion, my close friend, with whom I once enjoyed sweet fellowship?" (verses 13-14).

Verses 6-8: When betrayed, what action was David tempted to take?

Verses 16-18, 22-23: Where did David ultimately turn for comfort and healing?

2. If you have committed betrayal at some point in your life, compare your experience with that of David.

Ask yourself: What did I do . . . or what can I do . . . to remedy the betrayal I committed?

Confused:
What Is God Doing?

SENSING GOD'S CALL ON HIS LIFE, JIM RESIGNED HIS JOB AS AN ELECTRI-
cal engineer and took a position as a youth minister in a suburban
church. His love for Jesus and dynamic personality attracted many kids to
the youth group, and many of their young lives were dramatically changed.
At a summer camp Jim met an elementary school teacher named Emily.
After dating for a year they married.

Because of his exceptional giftedness, Jim received offers from other
churches. He felt led to accept the position of youth director in a large met-
ropolitan church. Jim wrote a book on ministry to teenagers and was in
demand as a seminar and retreat speaker. The couple was excited when they
learned that they would have a child, and the birth of baby Josh brought
even greater joy to them.

As the months passed Emily became ill. Unfortunately, Emily had
developed serious complications during her pregnancy that had required a
blood transfusion. The couple was shocked when tests revealed that Emily
had contracted the HIV virus from the transfusion of infected blood. They
had baby Josh tested, which showed that he too had the HIV virus. Jim and
Emily felt called to ministry, but what was God doing in their lives?

One day the chairman of the church board visited Jim and Emily at
home. Pressed by church members, he asked Emily not to use restrooms in
the church. Jim continued to serve effectively, but just before his third
birthday Josh died from AIDS. And then a few months later, the senior
pastor called Jim into his office. "I have both good news and bad news," he
said. "The good news is that you are doing a fantastic job with the youth.
The bad news is that you must resign."

"Why?" Jim asked, stunned. The pastor said that many church members felt uncomfortable around Emily, who now had AIDS. Unbelievably,
Jim and Emily were more certain than ever about their call to ministry, but
they were confused and distressed by their circumstances.

Jim got a part-time job at a hospice where he helped care for Emily
while they processed all that was happening to them. Before Christmas
Emily died from AIDS. Jim was heartbroken over the death of both his

wife and son and was confused about the loss of his ministry position.

In all this tragedy, what is God up to?[1]

Disciples in the Upper Room

John 13:31-16:33

The disciples left everything to follow Jesus: families, homes, and occupations. For three years they'd been His closest companions. Just a few days earlier they shared in the euphoria of Jesus' triumphal entry into Jerusalem—like NFL Super Bowl champions at a victorious homecoming parade. Now the disciples gathered in the Upper Room to eat the Passover meal together, its symbolism hauntingly pointing to Jesus' passion.

Jesus dropped a bombshell in their midst, saying that one of the disciples would disown Him (see John 13:38) and another would betray Him to His enemies (see 13:21). Even as the Lord spoke, the religious authorities were plotting His arrest. Reclining at the table in the flickering light of oil lamps, Jesus told the eleven even more devastating news. Soon He would have to leave them, He said, adding, "In a little while you will see me no more" (16:16). Sadly He said, "Where I am going, you cannot follow now" (13:36). Suddenly, the disciples' world fell apart. They'd hoped to share in a prosperous kingdom on earth with Messiah Jesus and now their expectations were shattered. They were "troubled" (14:1), "filled with grief" (16:6), and in "anguish" (16:21). Jesus added that in the days and weeks to come, "You will weep and mourn" (16:20) and "be scattered, each to his own home" (16:32). The disciples were utterly confused as to what God was doing in this sudden turn of events.

Following the meal, Jesus shared with the disciples His tender goodbye. Jesus' farewell speech is unlike any other Scripture. Rather than a logical series of propositions, "it is more like a musical composition. The composer tries to inspire the listener by the repetition of themes. Each time the same melody is played in a different setting, it is blended with other elements . . . The recurrence imprints the themes in his soul."[2] The melody of the Upper Room discourse announces Jesus' departure. The several themes proclaim God's provisions for the confused and distressed disciples.

To help them face and deal with their anguish, the Lord shared with His distraught disciples these comforting words:

"The Father and the Son love you deeply"
(14:21,23; 15:9; 16:27; 17:23).

Jesus told His friends that in spite of their darkness and confusion, they are infinitely and eternally loved. The Father loves them to the same degree that He loves His only Son; and the Son loves them with the same intensity that He is loved by the Father. They are loved profoundly—even Peter, who would deny Jesus with oaths and curses; even Judas, who would hand Him over to death.

"The Father has wedded you to Himself forever" (15:16; 17:2,6,9,12,24).

Before the universe was created, the Father chose them to be His children: "You did not choose me, but I chose you" (15:16). Seven times in this discourse Jesus stated that the Father gave the disciples to the Son as His possession: "They were yours; you gave them to me" (17:2). Soon Jesus would return to the Father to make ready rooms for them in the heavenly home—rooms of love, warmth, and safety. The promise of being with Jesus forever brought them great comfort.

"I will come to you in a new way through the Spirit" (14:16-19,23,26; 15:26; 16:7).

Following His immanent demise, Jesus would return to the Father and no longer be physically with them. But His departure would not signal the end of His presence: "I will not leave you as orphans; I will come to you" (14:18). Jesus would be with the disciples in a radically new way through another— even the Spirit—the personal and powerful presence of God. Under the Old Covenant the Spirit was *with* God's people (see Psalm 51:11); but following Jesus' exaltation, the Spirit would be *in* God's people: "You know him, for he lives with you and will be in you" (14:17). The Comforter would recall Jesus' words (see 14:26), guide them into all truth (see 16:13), and correct them when they stray (see 16:8). In Jesus' absence the Holy Spirit would be their spiritual director, forming them into the Master's image.

"The Father lovingly prunes you" (15:1-2).

Jesus presented the imagery of the Father as the gardener, Himself as the vine, and believers as the branches. The gardener lovingly prunes the living branches to promote their growth, and thus the most fruitful vines are those that are carefully trimmed. Much of the disciples' pruning will occur by opposition from the fallen world system (see 15:18-21; 16:2-4; 17:14). But all the pain and confusion the disciples feel will work for their ultimate good (see Romans 8:28). But as R. Kent Hughes noted, "God's hand is never closer than when he prunes the vine."[3]

"I will be praying for you in heaven" (17:9,15,20-26).

As He was about to leave His friends, Jesus promised to pray for them in their crises and confusion. He prayed that His followers might be united in faith and love (see verses 11, 21-23), that they might be set apart for God and His service (see verses 17-19), and that they might be protected from the vicious attacks of the evil one (see verse 15). Jesus promised to pray for His children right up to the time He says, "Welcome home!"

Jesus Ministers Spiritual Direction

CONSIDER HOW JESUS ministered spiritual direction to His confused followers in the Upper Room.

Jesus understood the anguished mood of His friends.

Because the Son of God lived a fully human life (though without sin) He feels our shattered dreams and confusion. The Lord mirrored back to the disciples their distress, anguish, and grief. As the writer to Hebrew Christians later put it, "We don't have a priest who is out of touch with our reality. He's been through weakness and testing, experienced it all—all but the sin" (Hebrews 4:15, MSG).

Jesus ministered to His disciples with tenderness and compassion.

Jesus' servant-act of washing the disciples' feet (see John 13:1-17) was an expression of sheer compassion. Showing His love for His friends struggling with confusion and pain infused them with courage and hope for the future. Jesus reinforced this by addressing the disciples as "dear children," *teknia* (13:33, NLT, MSG). The Lord's compassion made an indelible impression on John, the "beloved disciple," for seven times in his first letter John addressed Christian readers by the same endearing word for "dear children" (see 1 John 2:1,12,28; 3:18; 4:4; 5:21).

Jesus actively comforted the confused and distraught disciples.

Jesus reassured His friends of His constant love, His efficient prayers, and His unfailing protection. When the disciples felt most vulnerable, Jesus told them He would not leave them orphans, but would live in them through the Spirit. He assured them that their security lies with the Father, their unending life with the Son, and their final consolation with the Spirit. He promised them an unshakable home in heaven.

Jesus ministered with candid realism.

The Lord shared with His followers both the "bad" news and the good news. The Lord never shaded or colored the truth. He told them about His impending death, Peter's denial, and Judas' betrayal. He told them about the powers of evil at work in a world that would hate and persecute them.

But He also told them about His resurrection from the dead and eternal life in the Father's home. The good news of His victory over sin would overcome the "bad" news of their persecution and pain.

From Confusion to Certainty

IN THE UPPER Room Jesus also told His bewildered disciples what they must do to gain perspective and go forward in God's will. Again Jesus presented His teaching in the same form as a musical composition. The several themes indicate the spiritual responses they must make to appropriate His love and care.

We can trust God completely (see 14:1,11-12).
In the midst of their confusion, the disciples must trust God implicitly, as a child trusts its parent. Trust involves clinging to and committing one's total being to Jesus, who can bear the heaviest burdens. Like Thomas, we may not know the way we should take (see 14:5); like Philip, we may have lost sight of God in life's maze (see 14:8). But having trusted Jesus with our eternal destiny, we may confidently trust Him with the perplexities of our lives. The more we trust Jesus, the more the divine life opens up to us.

We can abide in the Lord as our home (see 14:23; 15:4-9).
Nine times in John 15:4-10, Jesus urged His followers to remain in Him, even as a vine and its branches are bound together in a single organism. Grafted into the vine by faith, we must continue to dwell in the life of Jesus. We must make Jesus the air we breathe, the water we drink, the bread we eat, the lamp that lights our lives. Jesus promised that if we abide in Him, "I will remain in you" (15:4)—with all the reassurance and hope this relationship affords.

We can cling to Him in prayer (see 14:13-14; 15:7; 16:23-24).
"I tell you the truth, my Father will give you whatever you ask in my name" (16:23). Prayer that begins as conversation, that unfolds as communion, and that deepens in contemplation pushes us into the presence of the Almighty. C. S. Lewis wrote, "Prayer in the sense of petition, asking for things, is a small part of it; confession and penitence are its threshold, adoration its sanctuary, the presence and vision and enjoyment of God its bread and wine. In it God shows himself to us."[4] Vital prayer goes a long way to clearing the confusion of our lives.

We can obey Him fully (see 14:15,21,23; 15:10,14).
"You are my friends if you do what I command" (15:14). Disciples must obey Jesus' commands amidst life's difficult challenges. John cherished this truth, for he later wrote: "If anyone obeys his word, God's love is truly made complete in him" (1 John 2:5). Jesus promised that the person who obeys Him would be filled with His comforting love. The degree to which we trust and obey is the degree to which God is free to reveal Himself in our lives. As Van Kaam puts it, "The more I keep your word, the more I become that word."[5] Jesus may not be experientially real to some Christians because of a lack of obedience.

We can give and receive love in the bond of unity (see 13:34-35; 15:12-13,17; 17:11,21-23).
The Old Covenant commanded love for others, with the words, "love your neighbor as yourself" (Leviticus 19:18). Under the New Covenant, Jesus lifted the bar of love's demand, saying, "A new command I give you: Love one another. As I have loved you, so you must love one another" (John 13:34; see also 15:12). God commands that we love others with the same self-giving compassion with which Christ loves us. Loving as Jesus loves means seeking others' good above one's own, not retaliating when wronged and, if necessary, laying down one's life for a friend (see 15:13).

We must give and receive love in the body of Christ—the community where brothers and sisters are one—as Father, Son, and Spirit are one in the unity of the Godhead (see 17:21). As we give and receive love in the body, God's light will clarify our confusion (see 1 John 4:12).

We can take courage and not lose heart (see 14:1,27; 16:33).
Jesus concluded His tender farewell by saying that if His disciples follow these directions they would flourish spiritually. (1) They will experience peace—even the peace Christ experienced amidst the storms of life (see 14:27; 16:33). (2) Their hearts will be filled with a joy—even the joy Jesus experienced doing the Father's will (see 15:11; 16:20-24; 17:13). (3) Christ's followers will not stray from the path of life (see 16:1). (4) The service of their hands will be fruitful and enduring (see 15:8,16). And supremely, (5) God will be glorified (see 15:8). His character and honor will be exalted, such that grateful praise will arise to Him.

A PRAYER

LORD, in life's trying circumstances I'm sometimes perplexed and distressed at what You're up to in my life and in the wider world. Help me not to lose heart, but to cling to Your encouraging promises and obey Your wise and loving directions. Help me hold tightly to Your powerful hand.

TRY IT YOURSELF

1. Take time to ponder the ways of God.
Recall a time of confusion or perplexity when you struggled to reconcile your experience in the world with what you know about the goodness of God in your head.

2. Ask yourself:
How did I react in that situation?

How was my reaction different from what Jesus called the disciples to do?

What spiritual lessons did I learn about God and His provisions from this experience?

Fearful

VICTOR WAS A LAY PASTOR IN AN UNDERGROUND CHURCH IN AN EAST-ern European country. A bold witness for Christ, Victor was interrogated and fined many times by the secret police. During a business trip to another city, he was taken into custody by the police and charged with selling Bibles and Christian books—material that was on the state's prohibited list. The two "witnesses" that reported Victor were conscripted by the secret service to lie about his activities, and as a result, Victor was tried and sentenced to three years in prison. The church covenanted to support Victor's family with their prayers and finances.

Four armed guards led Victor handcuffed and in leg chains into the lightless depths of the prison. The place was constructed of thick concrete walls and was cold, dark, and smelly—almost medieval. As they passed through dank corridors toward the cell, the atheist guards cursed Victor for his Christian faith. As they approached the cell, Victor saw a tiny, filthy cubicle with no windows. Rats scurried out of the dark corners of the cell that would be his home. As the guards opened the steel door to the cell, Victor was overcome with fright. For a split second he thought that a lion might charge out of that foreboding place. If his hands and feet had not been bound he would have fled. He was terrified at the thought of spending three long years in that hole.

Once the door was locked behind him, Victor fell to his knees and prayed earnestly to the Lord. A month later a sympathetic guard smuggled a pocket New Testament into his cell. Victor read the Scriptures and prayed for hours each day. As he did, the mighty presence of God filled his cell.

Victor's fear vanished, and his heart was filled with a profound sense of God's love and peace.

How can we find comfort, and direction for our souls, when fear imprisons us in spiritual darkness and God seems utterly absent?

Frightened at the Tomb

Matthew 28:1-10; Mark 16:1-8; Luke 24:1-8
While Jesus hung on the cross, a number of women looked on in horror from a distance (see Matthew 27:55-56). Three days later, as dawn was

breaking on Easter Sunday, a few of these women—including Mary Magdalene, the other Mary, and Salome—went to the sepulcher on a mission of love to anoint Jesus' body with spices. Women were the last to leave the cross Friday evening and the first to arrive at the tomb Sunday morning. Mary Magdalene, in particular, faithfully stood by Jesus from the time of her healing (see Luke 8:2). The male disciples had all retreated to their homes and occupations.

As the women approached the tomb, they were overcome with fear. They had been through many unsettling events: Jesus' arrest, His trials, and the Crucifixion itself. As followers of Jesus, their own lives were in danger. What might the Jerusalem power brokers do to *them*? As they approached the tomb "a violent earthquake" (*seismos*) shook the ground (Matthew 28:2).

A powerful earthquake itself is a frightening event. But in this case, there was more to terrify them. We read that an angel of the Lord descended from heaven, rolled back the stone that sealed the sepulcher, and sat upon it—a show of defiance and strength. The angel's "appearance was like lightning, and his clothes were white as snow" (Matthew 28:3). The tough sentries guarding the tomb were so frightened they couldn't move.

The grieving women's faces became white with fear. Mark reports that they were "alarmed" (*ekthaubeomai*, Mark 16:5), "trembling," "bewildered" (*ekstasis*, literally, "beside themselves"), and "afraid" (verse 8). They were so terrified, in fact, they couldn't speak.

The angel said to the stunned women, "Do not be afraid, for I know that you are looking for Jesus, who was crucified. He is not here; he has risen, just as he said. Come and see the place where he lay" (Matthew 28:5-6). Dropping their spices, the women ran through the cemetery to tell the others about the empty tomb. Matthew tells us that they were "afraid yet filled with joy" (Matthew 28:8).

Suddenly the risen Jesus appeared before the frightened women. John reports that Mary thought the stranger was a gardener (see John 20:15). (As an aside, a twelfth-century painting depicts Jesus as a gardener standing with shovel in hand.) Jesus tenderly called the lead character by name: "Mary." Recognizing the Lord, the women "clasped his feet and worshiped him" (Matthew 28:9). They clung to Jesus fearing that He might again be taken from them. They worshiped because they were thrilled to see Him alive. Sensing their fear, Jesus said, "You're holding on to me for dear life! Don't be frightened like that" (verse 10, MSG).

The risen Lord then commanded the women: "Go and tell my brothers to go to Galilee; there they will see me" (verse 10). Even though His disciples had given up hope and fled, Jesus held them near to His heart as "my brothers."

Jesus Ministers Spiritual Direction

THE RISEN LORD ministered soul care to the faithful but frightened women in several ways.

Jesus sent angels to instruct and comfort them.

Jesus ministered comfort to the women in the hour of their greatest fear. The Lord, who promised to come alongside His disciples through the Comforter (see John 14:16), here eased their fear through comforting angelic ministers (see Hebrews 1:14). The heavenly messenger told the frightened women the truth. Not just *words*, but the *truth*, to comfort. Speaking the truth is the first step to healing and freedom.

Jesus led the terrified women into the presence of God, where fright dissolves in the warmth and strength of divine love.

Jesus loved the women too much to leave them stricken with fear and "beside themselves." He came to them as the living answer to their urgent need. The fear that shook them to the core of their beings vanished in the comforting presence of the living, conquering Lord.

Jesus empowered the women to experience healthy fear, or reverential awe, of God.

When the women met Jesus, they "worshiped him" (Matthew 28:9). After seeing Jesus alive, the women were empowered to exchange servile fear for godly fear. Once frightened by the supernatural phenomena, they now stood in awe and reverence of Jesus, who had overcome the ultimate enemy—death.

Jesus gave the fearful male disciples the courage to believe that no failure is beyond forgiveness and repair.

Failing to trust Jesus fully and fearing for their own lives, the disciples fled following His arrest. When Jesus had risen from the dead, He sought out His shaken friends and ministered to them forgiveness, restoration, and courage.

Overcoming Fear

FEAR IS ONE of the most powerful and unsettling of human emotions. The more than five hundred references to fear in the Bible suggest that fear is a huge issue for us. With Augustine, we identify two kinds of fear: "servile fear" and "chaste fear."[1]

The first, destructive (or servile) fear, involves terror or fright. The second, constructive (or chaste) fear, is "the fear of the Lord," that involves reverence, awe, and heartfelt worship of God. The Bible commands the latter fear: "Serve the LORD with reverent fear, and rejoice with trembling" (Psalm 2:11, NLT). The radical difference between servile fear and godly fear is seen in Isaiah 8:12-14 (NLT): "Do not be *afraid* that some plan conceived behind closed doors will be the end of you. Do not *fear* anything except the LORD Almighty. He alone is the Holy One. If you *fear* him, you need *fear* nothing else. He will keep you safe" [emphasis added]. (The two forms of fear are also seen in Matthew 10:28.)

A little bit of fright is a good thing; it alerts us to potential dangers and fosters self-preservation. But when fear of persons or events fills us with anxiety and dread, it becomes destructive. Some may fear God in an unhealthy way. We may view God as a cosmic bully who is out to beat us with a club. We may fear that by obeying God we will lose our real selves. Servile fear cripples creative living, closes off communion with God, and allows Satan a foothold into our lives. Our natural response is to avoid or flee what we fear.

Henri Nouwen shares his experience of servile fear in this way:

> Even my best theological and spiritual formation had not been able to completely free me from a Father God who remained somewhat threatening and somewhat fearsome . . . Somehow, God's love for me was limited by my fear of God's power, and it seemed wise to keep a careful distance even though the desire for closeness was immense. . . . This paralyzing fear of God is one of the great human tragedies. . . . The final stage of the spiritual life is to so fully let go of all fear of the Father that it becomes possible to become like him. As long as the Father evokes fear, he remains an outsider and cannot dwell within me.[2]

How should Jesus' followers respond to paralyzing, servile fear?

We can identify the fear that assails our souls.

By naming the fear you are able to assess its dangers and address it in a redemptive way. Unidentified fear steadily grows and eventually overcomes us. Someone has said that fear begins as a small trickle of doubt that flows into the mind and eventually wears such a great channel that all our faith runs into it.

We can surrender the fear to God in prayerful trust.

Trust God with whatever strikes fear in your heart. David wrote, "When I am afraid, I will trust in you" (Psalm 56:3). We are not alone in a threatening universe. God is there to protect (see Deuteronomy 1:29-30), provide (see 1 Peter 5:7), and be present with His people always (see Hebrews 13:6). Psalm 112:7-8 says of the person who surrenders his fears to God: "He will have no fear of bad news; his heart is steadfast, trusting in the LORD. His heart is secure, he will have no fear." Or as one with this understanding said: "Fear knocked at the door. Faith answered. No one was there" (anonymous).

We can meditate on Scriptures that affirm the height, breadth, and depth of God's love.

The soul draws strength from the biblical truth that I am eternally loved by God. Don't make the mistake of measuring God's love for you by the measure of your love for God. Drink in biblical reminders of God's infinite love *for you*. For example: "Do not be afraid, for I have ransomed you. I have called you by name; you are mine . . . I am the LORD . . . your God . . . you are precious to me . . . and I love you" (Isaiah 43:1-4, NLT). "I have loved you with an everlasting love; I have drawn you with loving-kindness" (Jeremiah 31:3). And, "How great is the love the Father has lavished on us, that we should be called children of God" (1 John 3:1).

We can personally enter into the calming and reassuring presence of Almighty God.

Carve out a quiet space and permit the all-powerful and compassionate God to embrace you. A child's fears are calmed by being wrapped in a parent's arms; so the Christian's fears dissolve in God's presence. Paul tells us, "God has not given us a spirit of fear . . . but of power, love, and self-discipline" (2 Timothy 1:7, NLT). The positive embrace of God's power and love in the heart puts fear to flight. As John wrote, "There is no room in love for fear. Well-formed love banishes fear" (1 John 4:18, MSG).

Worship the Savior, and you will be freed from the tyranny of fear and dread. Fear Him, and you will not be terrorized by what man can do to you. "Do not fear anything except the LORD Almighty. He alone is the Holy One. If you fear him, you need fear nothing else" (Isaiah 8:13-14, NLT). Anxious fear is a sign that the soul is out of touch with God.

Hear Henri Nouwen again:

To those who are tortured by inner or outer fear, . . . Jesus says:
"You have a home; I am your home; Claim me as your home;
You will find it to be the intimate place where I have found my
home; It is right where you are in your innermost being, in your
heart."[3]

We can remember that we don't have to go very far to find the antidote to servile fear.

The remedy for destructive fear is Jesus and His immense love. As a line of a familiar hymn puts it, "Jesus the name that calms our fears, that bids our sorrows cease." Struggling with fear and loneliness, David wrote, "The LORD is my light and my salvation—whom shall I fear? The LORD is the stronghold of my life—of whom shall I be afraid?" (Psalm 27:1)

See Jesus in your most fearful places. A critically ill saint in a hospital room does well to contemplate Jesus sitting on the edge of the bed, intimately sharing words of comfort and hope.

A Prayer

O God of comfort, help me make the heartfelt cry of Augustine the prayer of my own soul: "Lord, you have saved my soul from the constraint of fear, so that it may serve you in the freedom of love."[4]

Try It Yourself

1. **Search the Scriptures.**
   Identify several other occasions in the Gospels where Jesus said, "Do not fear" or "Don't be afraid."

   What struck fear into the hearts of the persons to whom Jesus spoke these comforting words?

   Have you felt anxious or fearful of some of these issues yourself—poor health, rejection, or assault by evil spirits? Write them down on paper.

2. **As you come into Jesus' presence, release these fears to the Lord, knowing that He wants you to fear – that is, reverence and worship – only Him.**

Discouraged and Despairing

FOR MANY YEARS, CHRISTIANS IN AFGHANISTAN WERE A PITIFULLY SMALL minority. But through Christian missionary work and the discreet witness of the handful of Christians, more Afghanis became followers of Jesus. Although there were no visible churches in the country, believers met secretly in small groups to worship, study the Scriptures, and encourage one another.

The church in Afghanistan had reason to be encouraged. The population was disillusioned with Islam and was quietly looking for answers, so many ordinary people were willing to give the gospel a secret hearing. Believers were excited when in 1972 the Afghan government allowed a Christian place of worship to be built in the capital. Soon thereafter the monarchy fell, which Christians interpreted as a sign that God was defending His cause.

But events took a dark turn. The repressive socialist regime that came to power fostered the strictest interpretation of the Koran. The Christian house of worship was demolished as disrespectful to Islam. In the years that followed, the Soviets invaded Afghanistan in what would become a decade-long conflict of bloodshed and starvation. For the small band of Jesus' followers, life became nearly intolerable. The Bible, church music, and Christian films were burned. Proselytizing an Afghanistan citizen drew the sentence of death.

In the face of severe repression, the handful of believers despaired. They had believed that God was on His throne and that, however slowly, the kingdom was being built in that part of the world. But the flickering light of the gospel was being extinguished by a growing spiritual darkness. "Why after so many years of oppression," the handful of believers asked, "has God not intervened and vindicated His cause?" Some Christians fled the country, seeking a better life elsewhere.

What *was* God doing, or was He gone too?

Two Disciples on the Emmaus Road

Luke 24:13-35
On the very first Easter afternoon Cleopas and another disciple—perhaps his wife—journeyed seven miles from Jerusalem to their home in Emmaus.

The two were part of the wider circle of Jesus' disciples who viewed the crucifixion from the shadows. Walking along the road, their thoughts were still
at Calvary as they struggled to make sense of what had happened. Then Jesus
overtook them and became their secret companion on the way.

The stranger asked the pair, "What are you discussing together as you
walk along?" (verse 17). The disciples stopped in their tracks, "their faces
downcast" (verse 17). Their sullen countenances revealed their desperate
state of mourning the dead prophet they had followed. Cleopas expressed
amazement that the stranger was unaware of the terrible things that had
occurred in Jerusalem. The stranger replied, "What things [happened]?"
(verse 19). Jesus knew their state of mind; but by inviting the two to talk
He gave them opportunity to release their disappointment and despair.

A week earlier when Jesus entered Jerusalem, the disciples with the
crowd cheered Him as King of Israel (see John 12:12-13). But the One they
hoped would liberate the nation from its Roman captors was brutally exe-
cuted. Their hero was dead, His mission a failure, their hopes dashed. With
the collapse of their dreams, the two disciples were confused and despondent. Women friends witnessed the empty tomb, and angels announced
that Jesus was alive. But after three days Jesus was nowhere to be found.
The disciples' hearts were torn between despair and hope.

As they walked and talked on the road, these disciples "were kept from
recognizing him" (verse 16). Why was this?

Unaware of the Scriptures that spoke of Messiah's resurrection, they had
no expectation of seeing Jesus again. Moreover, the dark cloud of dashed
hopes had dulled their awareness of His presence. Then too, the disciples
were traveling in the wrong direction—away from the fellowship of believers in Jerusalem. On their own, they were shortsighted and despairing.

The stranger gently reprimanded the pair for failing to understand the
Scriptures, which would have explained the tragic event that had just taken
place. Jesus' rebuke was tender but direct: "How foolish" (that is, "lacking
understanding") you are, and how slow of heart ("dull") to believe all that
the prophets have spoken!" (verse 25). The disciples failed to understand that
Messiah's appointed path to glory was paved with rejection and suffering.

The stranger then explained what the Scriptures teach about the
Messiah (see verse 27). He undoubtedly pointed them to the bruised but
victorious "seed" of the woman (see Genesis 3), the Passover lamb (see
Exodus 12:21), the scapegoat (see Leviticus 16), the suffering Servant (see
Isaiah 53), and the pierced victim (see Zechariah 12). Still they failed to
recognize the stranger in their midst.

As they came to Emmaus, "Jesus acted as if he were going farther" (verse
28). How Jesus must have longed to reveal Himself to the disciples and heal

their despair! Recognizing the stranger as someone special, they urged Him to stay the night at their home. Jesus immediately accepted their invitation—the Lord never refuses an invitation from a welcoming heart.

Eating and Seeing

As they sat at the table, Jesus seized the initiative. He gave thanks for the food, broke the bread, and offered it to the pair. The disciples thought they were inviting the stranger as a guest, but they were surprised to find that they were the stranger's guests, and He was their host! This symbolic act echoed the Last Supper that Jesus celebrated with the eleven a few days earlier.

Immediately the disciples' eyes were opened, and they recognized that the stranger at their table was the living Messiah. This remarkable incident suggests that Jesus is with His people in a special way as they remember His death at the Eucharistic table. Rosage offers a helpful insight: "Jesus led the two disciples into a contemplative experience of his divinity hidden in the breaking of the bread."[1]

Having revealed Himself to the ecstatic disciples, the risen Lord disappeared from their sight. God knew that Christ's presence through the Spirit is better than His physical presence. After meeting the risen Lord up close and personal, the pair couldn't keep the thrill to themselves. In spite of the darkness and the threat of bandits on the road, they set out for Jerusalem to tell the other disciples that the Lord is alive. They wanted the brothers and sisters to share in the incredible joy they discovered that evening.

Jesus Ministers Spiritual Direction

THE STORY OF the two disciples on the road to Emmaus offers fruitful spiritual guidance for the confused and despairing.

Jesus asked the despondent disciples probing questions.

The Lord didn't immediately lay out the solution to the disciples' despair. He gave them opportunity to talk; open-ended questions allowed the pair to unburden their hearts, verbalize their confusion, and air their disappointment. A person is not likely to grasp his real issues until he expresses them in words.

Jesus attentively listened with interest and concern.

He practiced active listening as the disciples shared their crushed hopes and demolished dreams. Attentive listening facilitates hearing the voice of the Spirit—the true spiritual director. Jesus showed that spiritual direction has an important nondirective component to it: listening to the directee's questing spirit and prayerfully waiting on the Spirit's leading. Jesus' listening presence to the pair in their need is an aspect of His priestly ministry.

Jesus offered timely correction and tender rebuke.
Jesus rebuked the disciples for their spiritual dullness (see verse 25), and He corrected their failure to grasp the necessity of His suffering and death (see verse 26). Jesus loved the disciples too much to leave them in their despair, and so gently wounded them in order to heal. Jesus' correction and rebuke illustrates the directive component of spiritual guidance. It also highlights an aspect of His prophetic ministry. Only after earning the disciples' trust in priestly fashion did the Lord minister to them prophetically.

Jesus instructed the disciples from Scripture.
He directed the distraught disciples to the inspired Word of God, which testifies to His person and reveals God's gracious provision for every human need (see verse 27). His skillful opening of the Scriptures (see verse 32) preceded the opening of the disciples' spiritual eyes (verse 31).

Jesus nourished the disciples with a life-giving revelation of Himself.
When Jesus expounded the Scriptures to the disciples on the road, their hearts "burned" within them (see verse 32). When He disclosed Himself to the pair in the breaking of bread, hope came alive. Their spiritual eyes opened, their blindness was healed, and the web of discouragement and despair was broken. Jesus delights to reveal Himself in ravishing beauty to forlorn followers. Once again we see Jesus' priestly ministry at work.

Jesus released the disciples to move forward with firm trust in God.
Once the disciples recognized the Lord, He promptly disappeared from their sight. Jesus knew that even redeemed human beings are too fragile to manage such a supernatural encounter for very long. Nevertheless, after experiencing Jesus' glorious presence the disciples were never the same. Having met the Lord, they were compelled to share the good news. The opening of their eyes (see verse 31) preceded the opening of their lips (see verse 35).

Despair and Hope

SCRIPTURE DEPICTS DESPAIR by words such as "anguish," "desolation," and "gloom." Despair and hope are opposite sides of the same coin, for the Latin word for despair *(desperatio)* means "without hope." The essence of despair is loss of hope in God and the future. This absence of God's reassuring presence qualifies as a legitimate "dark night of the soul" experience.

Because God has commanded us to "Rejoice in the Lord always" (Philippians 4:4), Christian writers have identified despair as one of the seven principal vices. Hope, on the other hand, is one of the three theological virtues, along with faith and love (see 1 Corinthians 13:13).

As sinners in a fallen world, darkness and despair wash over all of us now and again. Great Christians such as Martin Luther, John Donne, and Søren Kierkegaard experienced troublesome bouts of depression and despair. Many biblical persons also experienced seasons of despair, including Job (see Job 3:3-19), Elijah (see 1 Kings 19:3-4), David (see Psalms 22, 69), Jeremiah (see Jeremiah 20:14-18), and Judas (see Matthew 27:3-5; Acts 1:18). Unhealed, "despair can sour into bitterness, resentment, [and] a self-perpetuating self-pity."[2]

But tasting despair can be the catalyst for transformation in Christ. Teachable souls that sink to the depths often rise to the heights of Christlikeness and fruitfulness.

How can a child of God who is afflicted with despair recapture life and hope? Here are a few principles emerging from this episode, and other Scriptures.

We can ask the question, "What good purpose might God be working in my life through this dark and painful experience?"

Scripture gives us the confidence that God relentlessly works for the good of His children and the furtherance of His purposes (see Romans 8:28). Pain is often the precursor of new life and hope.

We can open our heart to God's overflowing and life-giving grace.

Martin Luther joyfully discovered that God's grace lifted him from the pit of despair: "Just when I was in death's deepest throes and had the least hope the Lord came . . . and by a miracle led my life out of death and destruction."[3]

The Holy Spirit is trustworthy to minister the grace of encouragement and hope to discouraged hearts.

We can seek the support of the community of believers who will minister to us as "little Christs."[4]

As we walk hand in hand with other believers and allow them to minister grace to us, we find the courage to rise above our discouraging circumstances. It's virtually impossible to nourish and sustain hope in isolation from the community of faith.

We can go forward with faith and courage.

An effective antidote to discouragement is the faith-act of taking courage. The link in Scripture between overcoming discouragement by taking courage is clear—Joshua said to the Israelites: "Do not be afraid; do not be discouraged. Be strong and courageous" (Joshua 10:25). David, similarly, said to Solomon: "Be strong and courageous. Do not be afraid or discouraged" (1 Chronicles 22:13).

We can seek out a spiritual friend or director who will support us in the recovery of confidence, hope, and joy.
As Jesus served as an effective spiritual guide to the despondent disciples, so God graciously provides supportive spiritual friends who minister Christ and hope to struggling pilgrims today.

> For I know the plans I have for you, declares the LORD, "plans to prosper you and not to harm you, plans to give you hope and a future." (Jeremiah 29:11)

A PRAYER
When my life looks like a cratered pathway . . . when dark clouds extinguish hope . . . when I am sorely tempted to despair . . . help me to realize that You, O God, are my constant, never-failing, and strong companion.

TRY IT YOURSELF
1. Serve as a minister of encouragement and hope.
A survey by Gallup and Jones concludes that 22 percent of adults in the last twenty-four hours experienced dark moments of discouragement.[5]
Identify an acquaintance, friend, or family member who appears to be discouraged or who has lost hope.

2. With insights gleaned from this chapter, pray about how you might minister encouragement and hope to that person.
Then take the first step to being a messenger of grace to the person in need.
Henri Nouwen somewhere said, "Those who keep speaking about the sun while walking under a cloudy sky are messengers of hope, the true saints of our day."

Failure of Devotion

ANDY WAS AN INTENSE PERSON WITH A CHARMING PERSONALITY. He was the consummate salesman and leader and his father and grandfather had been pastors in a mainline denomination. So his parents and friends never doubted that in spite of his eccentricities Andy would enter the Christian ministry.

Andy attended seminary, spent a year as a vicar in the family parish, and then was ordained pastor of a newly organized independent church. The church had a humble beginning, meeting in an abandoned Laundromat. Within a few years the church grew to five hundred members and the pastor's reputation spread, such that out-of-town visitors often worshipped there. Andy became something of a tourist attraction. The flock revered him, certain he could do no wrong.

As the congregation continued to prosper, so did Andy. His lifestyle—home, cars, and exotic vacations—exceeded the generous salary the church paid him. His sermons became more perfunctory and his attention to people's needs less caring. Something clearly was amiss.

After months of questions, the rumors turned out to be true. Andy was embezzling church funds and was having an extramarital affair. When he was asked how a minister could do the things he was charged with doing, Andy replied, "I no longer believe that God stuff." A canker had slowly been eating at Andy's soul, causing him to deny the Lord he professed to serve.

Andy quit before the church could press charges. The immensity of his failure so overwhelmed him that he was unable to face anyone. He left his family, severed friendships and business acquaintances, and ended his romantic liaison. Andy soon left town and was never seen again. Rumors have it that he changed his name and is driving a delivery truck.

What spiritual direction does Jesus offer to those whose devotion to Him is failing?

Peter's Rise and Fall and Renewal

Matthew 26:31-35,69-75; John 21:15-23

Peter seemed to have it all together. He left everything to follow Jesus and made his way into the Lord's inner circle. When others were confused about Jesus' identity, Peter confessed Him as the Messiah and Son of God (see Matthew 16:16). Jesus blessed Peter for this insight, saying that he would be the "rock" upon which His church would be built (verse 18).

Later, in the Upper Room, Jesus predicted that all the disciples would desert Him. Peter brashly said he would never abandon his Lord: "Even if all fall away on account of you, I never will" (Matthew 26:33). So confident was Peter that he said, in effect, "No matter what, I will follow you. Count on me!" Jesus answered, "Before the rooster crows, you will disown me three times!" (verse 34). Persuaded he was strong enough for any trial, Peter said, "Even if I have to die with you, I will never disown you" (verse 35).

Peter's Denial

After being arrested later that night, Jesus was dragged to the house of Caiaphas, the high priest, for questioning. Peter was standing in the courtyard, warming himself near a fire. When a servant girl remarked that Peter had been with Jesus, the disciple protested, "I don't know what you're talking about" (verse 70).

As Peter retreated toward the courtyard gate, another young girl identified Peter as a follower of Jesus. Peter strongly denied this with an oath, saying, "I don't know the man!" (verse 72).

Other bystanders, alerted by his Galilean accent, also identified him as a follower of Jesus. With cursing and swearing Peter responded, "I don't know the man!" (verse 74). Immediately, a rooster crowed, as the Lord had predicted.

As Jesus was led back through the courtyard, He looked at Peter with sorrow and pity etched in His eyes. In a flash, Peter remembered the Lord's prediction and his own spirited avowal of faithfulness. The powerful fisherman had trembled before the words of a maidservant. Peter ran from the courtyard and wept in a flood of tears. Broken in spirit, his slow process of healing began.

Peter's Restoration

After Jesus' crucifixion the disciples returned to Galilee. A week later Jesus suddenly appeared to Peter and six other disciples by the Sea of Galilee. It happened this way . . .

Peter said to the others, "I'm going out to fish" (John 21:3). Still discouraged by his failure, Peter sought relief in the physical activity of fishing. The other disciples joined him in the boat, but that evening all the nets they pulled in were empty.

Early in the morning, Jesus appeared, standing onshore, and directed the disciples to a miraculous catch of 153 fish. Jesus then served the disciples a breakfast of broiled fish and hot bread. When Peter last stood by a fire, he shamefully denied his Lord. As he stood near the fire by the Sea of Galilee, powerful memories of that night swirled through his mind.

When they finished eating, the sun lifted above the horizon. Jesus motioned to Peter to join Him for a private talk. A profound sense of regret must have been stained on Peter's soul from his earlier failure of devotion. (Perhaps you can recall how badly it felt conversing with a person you had badly failed.)

Jesus said to Peter, "Simon son of John, do you truly love me more than these [do]?" (John 21:15). Jesus' question reminded Peter that his actions had fallen far short of his professions of loyalty. By calling him "Simon" — his name prior to becoming a follower — Jesus implied that the fallen disciple must make a fresh start with Him. Jesus' word for "love" *(agapaō)* implies the highest form of sacrificial love. Peter replied to Jesus' question, "Yes, Lord . . . you know that I love you" (verse 15). Peter's word for "love" *(phileō)* signifies the love of friendship or natural affection. Because of His cowardly denial and sense of failure, Peter couldn't claim to love Jesus with a consuming, sacrificial love.

Jesus asked him a second time, "Simon son of John, do you truly love me?" Again, Jesus used the word *agapaō.* Peter replied once more, "Yes, Lord, you know that I love you" (verse 16), using again the weaker word for love, *phileō.*

A third time Jesus asked Peter, "Simon son of John, do you love me?" (verse 17). This time Jesus used Peter's weaker word for love, *phileō.* Twice Jesus asked Simon if he loved Him with a deep, sacrificial love. The third time the Lord asked Simon if he loved Him with a brotherly love or natural affection.

Peter was upset (literally, "grieved") that Jesus posed the question a third time. His voice scarred with frustration, Peter replied, "Lord, you know all things; you know that I love you" (verse 17). Jesus' three questions by the seashore reminded Peter of his three denials in the courtyard. And the Lord's use of Simon's weaker word for love, *phileō,* brought him face to face with his failure of devotion.

In this way, Jesus' skillful probing gave Peter insight into his weakness, drained him of self-sufficiency, and forced him to examine honestly his relationship with the Lord.[1]

On that walk with Jesus along the beach, Simon died, but Peter was resurrected. Peter realized that he was infinitely loved, and he must love in return. Jesus erased Peter's three denials with three commands to shepherd the flock. Three years earlier Jesus called Peter to the work of an evangelist (see Matthew 4:18-19). By the Sea of Galilee, Jesus enlarged his call to include the work of a shepherd. As F. F. Bruce noted, "Now to the evangelist's hook there is added the pastor's crook, so that ... Peter proceeded to fulfill his double commission 'by hook and by crook.'"[2]

The results of Peter's restoration and transformation are seen in the book of Acts, where three thousand people were converted at his Pentecost sermon and by his courageous leadership in the early church. Peter's heartfelt love for Christ shines through his correspondence: "Though you have not seen him, you love him" (1 Peter 1:8)—Peter's word here is *agapaō*—heart-gripping, sacrificial love!

Peter's Commissioning

Walking along the lakeshore, Jesus told Peter what faithful discipleship would cost—martyrdom that would glorify God. Earlier, Peter brashly boasted that he would die for Jesus. Only now after Peter had been "rebirthed" did Jesus disclose the violent death he must die. Church fathers reported that Peter was crucified in Rome about A.D. 64, during Nero's brutal reign.

Hearing footsteps as they walked along the shore, Peter saw John following close behind. Peter asked, "Lord, what about him?" (John 21:21). Jesus replied, "If I want him to remain alive until I return, what is that to you? You must follow me" (verse 22).

The Lord assigned to Peter and John different callings and different endings to their stories. Peter, a man of action and leadership, would follow Jesus as a prophet and preacher; he would die as a martyr. John, a man of insight and reflection, would follow Jesus as a seer and poet; he would serve Christ to a ripe old age.

Jesus Ministers Spiritual Direction

JESUS' ENCOUNTER WITH Peter by the Sea of Galilee provides insights into His ministry of spiritual guidance to a fallen follower.

Jesus interceded for Peter.

Earlier, in the Upper Room, Jesus said, "I have prayed for you, Simon, that your faith may not fail" (Luke 22:32). Satan longed to destroy Peter, the leader of the early church, but Jesus' prayers shielded him from the worst of the Devil's attacks. Without Jesus' prayers, Peter might have followed the destructive path Judas trod.

Jesus allowed Peter to experience painful failure.

By denying his Lord, Peter's soul entered a barren desert. His failure, however, became a powerful occasion for self-examination and a catalyst for growth. Peter's love for, and devotion to, Jesus would be enlarged by his agonizing failure. Adrian Van Kaam notes, "To pierce our illusion, to deflate our arrogance, He may allow us to fail many times."[3]

Jesus posed questions to Peter that probed his motives and exposed his weaknesses.
Jesus' three soul-searching questions caused Peter to discover aspects of his character that he had not been in touch with. The Lord wouldn't settle for superficial answers, but pressed the question until Peter's heart was laid bare. Jesus' penetrating questions cracked the shell of the disciple's self-sufficiency and failure of devotion.

Jesus pursued a strategy of spiritual surgery that drained Peter of septic self-sufficiency, ego-drivenness, and unholy ambition.
Peter had to know himself in truth, face up to his brokenness, and experience Jesus' healing touch. Only then would he be prepared for God-honoring, apostolic ministry. Jesus dealt patiently with His fallen disciple, knowing that growth and healing may be painfully slow.

Jesus strengthened Peter's love.
Jesus brought Peter back to the first and greatest commandment of the Law, given to Moses fifteen hundred years earlier (see Deuteronomy 6:5) and reaffirmed by Himself: "Love the Lord your God with all your heart and with all your soul and with all your mind" (Matthew 22:37). Peter's heart had to be kindled with a deep passion for God. Nothing less than agape love would satisfy his heart and soul and sustain his service.

Jesus demonstrated that God's call upon each person is unique.
The Lord had one purpose for Peter and another purpose for John. Jesus taught that we must leave our brothers and sisters—their service and destinies—in God's loving hands. A disciple must not compare himself with another or with his circumstances. Sufficient is the evil in our own hearts.

Deficient Devotion

EVEN AS LEADER among the disciples, Peter was a saint in need of soul work. Though sincere of purpose and generous of heart, his character and spirituality were deficient. Peter was a man of quick talk ("Never Lord! . . . This shall never happen to you!" (Matthew 16:22)); impulsive action (he sliced off a slave's ear (see John 18:10)); proud self-confidence ("I will never disown you" (Matthew 26:35)); phony bravado (he attempted to walk on water (see Matthew 14:28-31)); self-seeking (he disputed who would be the greatest (see Luke 22:24)); and fickle devotion (he fell asleep in the Garden of Gethsemane (see Matthew 26:40-41,43,45)); and followed Jesus from afar (see Luke 22:54)) Peter was a man out of touch with his own brokenness.

At the core of his being, Peter lacked wholehearted connectedness to Jesus. Only a durable agape love for the Master would gird his life with stability and fidelity. But Peter's love was deficient (see John 21:15-17) and his faith feeble (Matthew 14:31). The divinity of Jesus that he confessed failed to captivate his soul. Hence Peter lived in his own strength and with a devotion that was less than pure.

The cunning adversary, who stalks like a lion, saw in Peter easy prey. Less than stable and lacking in love, Peter was vulnerable to the wiles of the Devil (see Luke 22:31-33). More of a sandcastle than a "rock," Peter crumbled—denying the Lord and damaging His cause.

Each of us, like Peter, is spiritually frail and a potential casualty, come crunch time. How can a Christian avoid the failure of devotion that brings discredit to the cause of Christ? Here are some suggestions that arise from Jesus' ministry to Peter.

We can recognize our inability to glorify the Lord in our own strength.

As Adrian Van Kaam, a gifted and godly spiritual guide, puts it, "The only thing I can do is disown You. It is arrogance to think that I can follow You anywhere, any way, any time on my own initiative."[4] An honest assessment of our weakness will lead to genuine humility and complete dependence on God.

We can be our authentic selves before God and others.

Don't pretend to be what you're not (strong, smart, or steady). Jesus chose real, not perfect, people as His followers. We all fail. But, "It is better to be a follower who fails than one who fails to follow."[5] When we do fall short, we can trust God's grace to rebuild our life. By faith and the practice of healthy spiritual habits, we allow God to mold us into the image of His Son.

We can honestly identify pockets of weakness and vulnerability in our life.

We can pray about potential self-deceptions as God brings them to our awareness. Twelve-step programs operate on the premise that recovery springs from honest acknowledgment of our brokenness. Being a Christian is no guarantee that there are no cankers in our soul needing healing. Bring these needs trustingly before the Lord in prayer. He specializes in radical forgiveness.

Above all, we can cultivate a relationship with Jesus that is deep rather than superficial, centered in the heart rather than limited to the head.

Like Peter, we need to love with agape power. This means loving God with all one's heart. By meditating on the Scriptures, abiding in His presence, and sharing with Him all our concerns, heart intimacy will grow. Lacking deep love relationship with God, we—like Peter—are a casualty waiting to happen. But we saw earlier (chapter 4) that living a life of love is the final stage of the spiritual journey.

A PRAYER

"Prone to wander, Lord, I feel it. Prone to leave the God I love."[6] Like Peter, Lord, my love is often deficient, my loyalty often lacking. May agape love for You so grip my heart that I continue to gladly stand up and be counted as a follower of the Carpenter of Nazareth.

TRY IT YOURSELF

1. Prayerfully reflect on a personal failure.

Create a quiet space and reflect on your life. It's unlikely that you have experienced a failure of devotion on the scale of Peter's. But whatever the nature of your failure, be assured that God remains in the business of forgiveness and restoration.

2. In a journal or notebook, describe an incident in which you failed the Lord.

Did you feel at the time that you had "blown" things so badly that God might never use you again?

How did God graciously bring about your restoration and renewal?

What lessons did you learn from this experience that might enable you to help others struggling with their own failures of devotion?

Anger and Rage

As far back as college days Sam was interested in issues of social justice. Appointed pastor of a small church on the West Coast, it wasn't long before he linked up with Right to Life groups in the area. His passionate zeal for the rights of the unborn caused him to assume leadership in the anti-abortion movement. The fact that millions of abortions were done each year filled Sam with righteous indignation. Nothing seemed to arouse his anger more than the taking of innocent lives in the womb.

The hometown newspaper gave front-page coverage to the fire that completely destroyed the local abortion clinic. After investigating the crime, the police charged Sam and two of his colleagues with arson. In court Sam pleaded guilty to setting the fire, but stated that his anger against the evil of abortion was morally justified. He must obey God rather than man, he told the judge. The abortion clinic arsonists were sentenced to two and a half years in prison.

Sam was released from prison after two years by reason of good behavior. His church welcomed him back as their pastor. Terms of parole restrictions forbade him from having any contact with anti-abortion or Right to Life groups. Those close to Sam following his release from prison found him unrepentant and as angry as ever against abortion doctors.

Within a year another abortion clinic in the area was torched. Sam was convicted again and sentenced to eight years behind bars. In an interview with the media before his return to prison, he said that his anger against abortion was so great that he would stop at nothing to eradicate this massive social evil.

Sam was much like another man who was also full of anger—a man for whom Jesus went to extraordinary lengths to offer spiritual direction.

Saul the Persecutor

Acts 9:1-9
Trained under the Orthodox rabbi Gamaliel, Saul was a brilliant Pharisee, zealous for Judaism and scrupulous regarding the Law. Saul first appears in Scripture at the stoning of Stephen, where he encouraged those who killed

the first Christian martyr (see Acts 7:58; 22:20). The sight of righteous Stephen praying for his killers undoubtedly haunted Saul through the years.

When persecution broke out against the church in Jerusalem, Christians scattered throughout Judea and Samaria. The Pharisee was a key player in the persecution: "Saul began to destroy the church. Going from house to house, he dragged off men and women and put them in prison" (Acts 8:3). The verb *destroy*, meaning "devastate" or "ravage," conjures the picture of a wild beast mangling its prey. A short time later, "Saul was still breathing out murderous threats against the Lord's disciples" (Acts 9:1). Saul was not only zealous for the Law, he was fuming with anger and rage against followers of the Way, who were growing in numbers and influence. Saul secured letters from the high priest authorizing him to arrest believers in Jesus and drag them back to Jerusalem, where they would be beaten, imprisoned, and in some cases, killed. Later, in his defense before Herod Agrippa, Paul testified that he tried to get the believers to "blaspheme" Christ and His teachings (26:11). He added, "In my obsession against them, I even went to foreign cities to persecute them" (verse 11)—the Greek participle, *emmainomenos,* translated *obsession* means "furious anger" or "boiling rage."

Nearing Damascus, where he sought to arrest disciples of Jesus, Saul was struck by a brilliant, flashing light from heaven that struck him to the ground and rendered him sightless. A voice said, "Saul, Saul, why do you persecute me?" (9:4). When Saul asked who was speaking, the heavenly stranger replied, "I am Jesus, whom you are persecuting" (verse 6). At Jesus' command Saul was led into Damascus, where a disciple named Ananias laid hands on Saul, after which he received the Holy Spirit and regained his sight. When Saul gave testimony to what Christ had done for him, saints in Damascus couldn't believe what they heard. They asked one another, "Isn't he the man who raised havoc in Jerusalem among those who call on this name?" (verse 21).

Saul, then, had persecuted the fledgling church with fury. The violence he vented against followers of the Way was driven by his white-hot anger, motivated by his zeal for the traditions of Judaism (see Galatians 1:14), and by his fear that this upstart "heresy" posed a serious threat to the form of Judaism he zealously defended.

Jesus Ministers Spiritual Direction

JESUS TOOK HOLD of Saul and transformed him from an angry persecutor of the church into a saintly apostle whose life was graced with goodness. How did Jesus minister spiritual direction to the Pharisee Saul, now become the apostle Paul?

Jesus led Paul into the desert where He ministered to the new convert for three years.

Before Paul consulted with Peter or other leaders in Jerusalem, Christ directed him into the desert of Arabia, where centuries earlier Moses and Elijah communed with God. In that solitary environment Paul prayed and deepened his relationship with the Savior. We can believe that in the desert Jesus showed Paul his overly zealous, angry self and performed spiritual surgery on his soul.

The Spirit of Christ enabled Paul to die to his sinful passions, including anger and rage.

The Spirit faithfully ministered to Paul through the years. To Timothy, Paul wrote, "Even though I was once . . . a persecutor and a violent man, I was shown mercy. . . . The grace of our Lord was poured out on me abundantly, along with the faith and love that are in Christ Jesus" (1 Timothy 1:13-14).

Paul's words "I have been crucified with Christ" (Galatians 2:20) indicate that he saw himself nailed, as it were, to the cross with Christ. The crucified Christ removed from Paul, at his conversion, the curse of sin and death. But Christ enabled Paul throughout his life to die to his old self and to be liberated from the power of his fleshly passions. Paul wrote, "We know that our old self was crucified with him so that the body of sin might be done away with, that we should no longer be slaves to sin" (Romans 6:6; see also Romans 8:13).

It was the Spirit of Christ who empowered Paul to die to his old way of life, with all its negative energy. No longer need Paul "gratify the desires of the sinful nature" (Galatians 5:16), including "hatred" and "fits of rage" (verse 20).

The Spirit of Christ kept Paul humbled through weakness.

Paul wrote, "To keep me from becoming conceited . . . there was given me a thorn in my flesh, a messenger of Satan, to torment me" (2 Corinthians 12:7). Whatever Paul's affliction, it was providentially given to keep him leaning on Christ and learning of him. Paul's physical "thorn" caused him to rely less on his own resources and more on the grace of Christ.

The Spirit enabled Paul to come alive to a new quality of life.

Paul also wrote, "Christ lives in me" (Galatians 2:20). United with Christ in His Resurrection (see Romans 6:5), Paul found that the supernatural life of God's Son was birthed in him by the Spirit. The negative drives and passions that once ruled his life gave way to the graces and virtues of Christ.

The Spirit brought forth in Paul gracious fruit—replacing anger with "love," "goodness," and "self-control" (see Galatians 5:22-23). Yes, the Apostle still struggled with his old nature (see his account of the battle in Romans 7:14-25), but the graces of Christ now became his ruling passion. When Paul himself faced hostility, persecution, and beatings—things he once inflicted on followers of Jesus—he no longer responded with anger and revenge.

A second century Christian writing, the Acts of Paul and Thecla, describe the apostle as small of stature, baldheaded, and bowlogged. It notes that Paul was "full of grace, for at times he looked like a man, and at times he had the face of an angel."[1] The grace and power of Christ transformed Saul, the devil, into Paul, an "angel."

Defusing Anger

THE POWERFUL EMOTION of anger often is a deadly foe of the spiritual life. The Old Testament alone contains nearly six hundred references to anger and wrath. To understand this common human emotion, we distinguish between constructive and destructive anger.

Anger in the form of righteous indignation is an appropriate response to sin and injustice in a moral universe. The holy and righteous God often is angered by human sin (see Deuteronomy 29:20-26; Psalm 74:1). Moses' anger burned when Israel worshipped the golden calf (see Exodus 32:19). Jesus expressed constructive anger when He drove money changers and sellers of goods out of the temple at the beginning of His ministry (see John 2:13-17) and again near its end (see Matthew 21:12-13). Paul knew constructive anger, for he wrote, "In your anger do not sin" (Ephesians 4:26). But by adding, "Do not let the sun go down while you are still angry, and do not give the devil a foothold" (verses 26-27), Paul inferred that constructive anger easily gives way to destructive anger.

The story of Sam and his anger against the abortion industry illustrates the difference. The killing of millions of fetuses in the womb justifies constructive anger, or righteous indignation. But crossing the line to burn or bomb an abortion clinic constitutes destructive anger.

Destructive anger—the passion that intends ill toward another—is a sin. Christians today oppose sins of the flesh, such as fornication, but often neglect sins of the spirit, such as anger. Classical Christian authorities, however, identified anger as one of the seven deadly sins. The early church theologian Basil (d. 379) put it bluntly: "Anger is a kind of temporary madness."[2] The desert father, Abba Agathon, said, "A man who is angry, even if he were to raise the dead, is not acceptable to God."[3]

What causes destructive anger to well up within us? Anger may be brought on by hurt (or threat of hurt) from another person, by frustration at having one's agenda challenged (not getting our way), or by dissatisfaction with one's life. Destructive anger that rises up to harm another gives Satan easy access to our lives (see Ephesians 4:26-27).

The Old Testament (see Ecclesiastes 7:9), Jesus (see Matthew 5:22), and Paul (see Galatians 5:20; Ephesians 4:26; Colossians 3:8) all warn against harboring destructive anger. Scripture states that anger is the root of a host of other sins (see Proverbs 29:22), including verbal abuse, marital conflict, broken friendships, physical assault, and murder (see Matthew 5:21-22). Destructive anger also harms the perpetrator himself, for as Jerome (d. 420) said, "No one heals himself by wounding another."[4] An angry person, moreover, is ill-equipped to minister mercy and grace to others. Destructive anger also wastes energy that ought to be channeled in a constructive direction. The following illustrates the origin and development of anger.[5]

Destructive Action (directed outward)

Hurt ➡ Anger ➡ Revenge ➡   or

Depression (directed inward)

How can we manage the anger that so easily gets out of control and injures others and ourselves?

We can face up to the anger within.

We need to admit that the anger exists, take responsibility for it, and not settle for the excuse, "The Devil made me do it!"

Next, we should identify the cause of the anger, be it a hurt, a threat, or a frustration.

Then we need to evaluate as objectively as possible the anger-causing situation. If our anger is caused by the actions of another person, we should try to see things from her perspective. It often helps to share dispassionately with the other person the reason for our hurt and anger.

We can confess our anger to God.

Because destructive anger is a sin, we should feel godly sorrow for it and be willing to confess anger to God and release it before it becomes a deeply rooted canker in the soul. The psalmist Asaph became angry and bitter when he saw the wicked prosper and the godly suffer; but he found perspective by expressing his hurt to the Lord and taking refuge in Him (see Psalm 73). Sharing our hurt and anger with a spiritual friend (see James 5:16) also helps to defuse the power of this negative emotion.

We can forgive the person whose action precipitated the anger.

A powerful way to defuse anger is to forgive and pray for the person we perceive has offended, hurt, or frustrated us. Jesus said, "If you forgive men when they sin against you, your heavenly Father will also forgive you. But if you do not forgive men their sins, your Father will not forgive your sins" (Matthew 6:14-15). We must forgive not three times, as the rabbis taught, nor seven times as Peter suggested, but without limit (see Matthew 18:21-22). Neil Anderson points out the Christlike quality inherent in forgiveness: "Forgiveness is agreeing to live with the consequences of someone else's sins."[6]

In 1981, a deranged man in a fit of rage shot Pope John Paul II as he rode in his automobile through a crowded city street. We can understand how the Pope might have become angry toward the intended killer. Instead, he visited the would-be assassin in prison, hugged him, and forgave him in Christ's name. What an example of Christian forgiveness.

We can supplant the fleshly response of anger with the fruit of the Spirit.

Paul, who as an unbeliever directed his anger and wrath against the church (and Christ), wrote: "The acts of the sinful nature" include "hatred" and "fits of rage" (see Galatians 5:19-20). He added, "I warn you . . . that those who live like this will not inherit the kingdom of God" (verse 21). We should pray that the Holy Spirit would bring forth in our life the peaceable fruit of righteousness, which includes "love," "kindness," "goodness," and "self control" (see verses 22-23). Freedom from anger will become a reality as we keep in step with the Spirit's working in our life (see verse 25).

We can refrain from anger and resist revenge by a deliberate act of the will.

Peter tells us that when the mob hurled insults at Jesus on the cross, He didn't respond with angry threats, but entrusted his soul to God (see 1 Peter 2:23). We must do likewise. Paul commands followers of Christ to "Get rid of all bitterness, rage and anger. . . . Be kind and compassionate to one another, forgiving each other, just as in Christ God forgave you" (Ephesians 4:31-32; see Colossians 3:8). God would not have commanded us to control our anger if it were impossible by an act of our will and with His help.

A PRAYER

Holy Father, where there is injustice and oppression help me to respond in a righteous way that seeks to rectify the wrong. But when unrighteous anger arises in my heart, help me to confess it to You before it injures others and causes sorrow and grief. May the compassionate life of Christ become a reality in my life.

TRY IT YOURSELF

1. The next time you are angry, defuse the destructive energy of your anger.

The next time you become angry in a destructive way (It may be as early as today!), reread this chapter and try to understand the dynamics of this powerful emotion. Identify the cause of your anger and seek to assess clearly the anger-producing situation.

Deliberately confess your anger, and perhaps intended revenge, to the Lord. In addition, share it with a spiritually sensitive friend.

2. Meditate on Psalm 37:8-9.

What specific steps will you take to lessen incidents of anger and revenge in the future?

Part 3

Jesus Receiving Soul Care

Nourishing Communion

WE'VE SEEN HOW JESUS PROVIDED SPIRITUAL GUIDANCE, OR SPIRITUAL direction, to family, friends, strangers, and adversaries. Not bound by political or social "correctness," the Lord ministered grace and growth to men and women, rich and poor, peasant and politician, priest and laity. Jesus was the spiritual guide par excellence, who pointed seekers to the living God and who nurtured their relationships with the Father.

But Jesus, the minister, also received ministry from family, friends, and especially from His Father in heaven. Jesus welcomed being nurtured Himself because, clothed with the longings and limitations of our humanity—sin excepted—everything human requires connections, including the Son of Man.

Nurture from Family and Friends

AS THE SON of Man, Jesus *grew* physically, mentally, emotionally, socially, and spiritually. As Luke put it, "Jesus grew in wisdom and stature, and in favor with God and men" (Luke 2:52). Mary and Joseph provided Jesus with love, nurture, and training during His formative years in the family home. They taught the young Jesus moral principles and social graces, and nourished Him from the Jewish scriptures and their rich Old Testament heritage.

As the Son of Man, Jesus also *suffered*. His ultimate suffering occurred on the cross, where for six hours He hung in excruciating pain to pay the price for sin (see Hebrews 2:10). But Jesus also suffered in the years prior to Calvary, as Hebrews tells us: "Although he was a son, he learned obedience from what he suffered" (5:8). The Lord was misunderstood by associates and mistreated by adversaries. Like any of us, in difficult times the Lord cherished the presence, support, and encouragement of a few close friends. The twelve men He chose as disciples became His "friends" (John 15:15). With them He interacted, dialogued, wept, and prayed. He was particularly intimate with an inner circle of three disciples: Peter, James and John.

When the specter of the Cross cast its dark shadow across Jesus' life, He sought the spiritual and emotional support of His eleven remaining disciples. As they celebrated the Last Supper together, Jesus said, "I have eagerly desired to eat this Passover with you before I suffer" (Luke 22:15). The verb *desired* indicates the deep longing of His soul for companionship and support. In the Upper Room Jesus told His friends the allegory of the vine and the branches (see John 15:1-17). He pointed out that apart from the life-giving vine, the branches are dead. But it is equally true that the vine without the branches is naked and vulnerable. As F. B. Meyer put it, "We are necessary to Christ. He cannot do without us. The Son wants sons; angels will not suffice."[1]

Before His arrest Jesus took the eleven to Gethsemane for support in His lonely struggle with the will of God and the powers of darkness. Taking Peter, James, and John inside the Garden, He shared with them His spiritual and emotional pain: "My soul is overwhelmed with sorrow to the point of death. Stay here and keep watch with me" (Matthew 26:38). Jesus urged His three close friends to uphold Him in prayer as He agonized over the cup filled with the world's sin.

A few days later as He hung on the cross, the Lord was supported by the love of His mother, His aunt Salome, the two Marys, and John, who stood by Him, sorrowing and praying (see John 19:25-27). Jesus was comforted by the loyal support of His women friends, in particular.

The well-intentioned male disciples, however, often failed to provide the support Jesus longed for. They were slow to grasp His divine Messiahship and mission of suffering. His close friends failed Him on critical occasions. In the Garden they fell asleep when they should have been keeping vigil; moments later Judas betrayed Him to His enemies; and when the Lord was arrested, "all the disciples deserted him and fled" (Matthew 26:56). Soon Peter would deny Jesus with oaths and curses. At crunch time, when Jesus needed His friends the most, they were not there for Him.

Nourishment from His Heavenly Father

JESUS DREW UNFAILING strength and direction from His heavenly Father. Luke's gospel stresses the humanity of the Son. It's not surprising then that Luke calls attention to Jesus' frequent communion with the Father in prayer.

During His first preaching tour in Galilee, "[a]t daybreak Jesus went out to a solitary place" (Luke 4:42) for quiet reflection and prayer. Jesus' preaching and miracle working attracted large crowds that wanted to make Him their folk hero. At such times, "Jesus often withdrew to lonely places and prayed" (Luke 5:16). Before calling twelve disciples, "Jesus went out to a mountainside to pray, and spent the night praying to God" (Luke 6:12). For Jesus, decision time always meant prayer time.

Following the miracle of the feeding of the five thousand, when the crowd wanted to make Jesus king by force, He put the disciples in a boat and sent the crowd away. "After he had dismissed them, he went up on a mountainside by himself to pray. When evening came he was there alone" (Matthew 14:23). Jesus refused to cave in to the political passions of the crowd, but retired to solitary places to draw wisdom and strength from His Father. Later, in the region of Caesarea Philippi, before questioning the disciples regarding His identity, Jesus prayed in private (see Luke 9:18).

A week later, while in prayer on a high mountain with Peter, James, and John, the Father reaffirmed His love for the Son (see Matthew 17:5). The Transfiguration must have been a soul-fortifying experience even for Jesus. Later, in Judea, "Jesus was praying in a certain place" (Luke 11:1). His disciples were so struck by the quality of Jesus' communion with the Father that they asked Him to teach them how to pray. Jesus proceeded to give them the pattern for prayer: "Father, hallowed be your name"— "Father" connoting the intimate and nourishing relationship He enjoyed with Abba.

Reginald Fuller explains:

Jesus lives in constant prayer and communication with his Father. When he engages in vocal prayer, he is not entering, as we do, from a state of non-praying into prayer. He is only giving overt expression to what is the ground and base of his life all along. He emerges from non-vocal prayer in order to show that the power he needs for his ministry . . . depends on the gift of God. It is through that prayer and communion and constant obedience to his Father's will that he is the channel of the Father's saving action.[2]

During His earthly ministry, Jesus pursued the Father's heart in prayer for the nurturing of His own soul. Jesus knew that He couldn't make it on His own. Thus, He often arose early in the morning or even spent entire nights in communion with His heavenly Father. Through regular seasons of prayer, Jesus found strength for His life and direction for His ministry. He said, "I live by the power of the living Father who sent me" (John 6:57, NLT). The Son of Man was an effective spiritual director because He received nourishing spiritual direction from His Father in the power of the Spirit.

If the Divine Son of God was totally dependent on the Father for nurture and direction, how much more are we humans who minister spiritual guidance?

TRY IT YOURSELF

Strengthen your support system.

If during His earthly sojourn Jesus sought spiritual and emotional support from family and friends, how much more do we need similar nurturing?

Make a list of people that, through thick and thin, form your personal support system.

If you lack sufficient soul friends (see Ecclesiastes 4:10), prayerfully consider how you might cultivate the friendship of those who will help bear your burdens.

Intimate Conversation

I F MATTHEW 6:9-13 IS THE "MODEL PRAYER" FOR THE DISCIPLES, JOHN
17 is properly the "Lord's prayer," because it's all about Jesus. Like our
Lord's discourse in John 14-16, this prayer resembles a musical composition, where leading themes are repeated and interwoven to form a symphony of praise and petition. Let's tune in to this intimate conversation
between the Son and His heavenly Father.

An Evening Encounter

John 17
Leaving the Upper Room under the light of the Passover moon, Jesus
poured out His heart to the Father in a stirring farewell prayer.

**Jesus communed with *God* on the most intimate terms, calling Him
"Father."**
Jesus took time to be with God, whom He called "Father," "Holy Father," or
"Righteous Father." Calling God "Father" would have shocked the ears of a
first-century Jew. Yahweh was understood to be so exalted that a devout Jew
would not pronounce the sacred name, and a scribe who wrote the name felt
compelled to take a ritual bath. But Jesus spoke of God in these most tender,
intimate, and loving ways. The ease with which Jesus used the term "a father"
testifies to the depth of nurturing intimacy Jesus enjoyed with Abba.

**Jesus drew nourishment from the unity that exists between the
Father and the Son.**
Listen to Jesus confess to the Father in a spirit of surrender and love, "All I
have is yours, and all you have is mine" (verse 10). Hear Him utter the
words, "Father; just as you are in me and I am in you" (verse 21). Jesus was
one with the Father and the Spirit in the unity of the eternal Godhead—
"as we are one" (verse 22). But relationally, during His earthly pilgrimage,
Jesus drew strength from fellowship with His heavenly Father; so He also
prayed, "I in them and you in me" (verse 23). In this John 17 prayer Jesus
expressed His need for nourishment through intimate conversation and
loving communion with Abba.

Jesus luxuriated in the soul-fortifying love of the Father.

In prayer Jesus tenderly uttered the words, "Righteous Father . . . I know you . . . " (verse 25). The word *know* signifies an experiential knowledge rooted in a deep, personal relationship. Through love, trust, and obedience Jesus knows the Father and basks in His nourishing love: "you loved me before the creation of the world" (verse 24, see also verses 23,26). Drinking in the Father's immeasurable love, Jesus was empowered to give His life in love to others.

The nurture Jesus received from Abba strengthened Him to complete His mission.

Soaking up the Father's love through prayerful communion allowed Jesus to glorify the Father (see verse 1). What does this mean? Augustine (d. 430) said it well: "Glory is the widespread fame of anyone accompanied by praise."[1] During three years of ministry Jesus manifested the Father and met the physical and spiritual needs of multitudes. Now Jesus drew strength in prayer, that He might manifest the Father's excellence through suffering and death. By virtue of His obedience unto death, many sinners would come to know and love His Father. Jesus declared, "I have made you known to them, and will continue to make you known in order that the love you have for me may be in them and that I myself may be in them" (verse 26).

Dependent on the Father

It might be thought that the incarnate Son possessed the resources to manage the impending crisis, that He needed no nurture and support from the Father as He faced betrayal and death. Far from it!

Without vital connectedness to the Father, the Son of Man could do nothing. So Jesus spent His last hours on earth in soul-nourishing conversation with Abba in prayer.

We must never forget that it's as a result of His nurturing relationship with the Father that the risen Jesus became the conduit through which the divine life and love flow to enrich the world.

And so it will always be with us. So also, only as we intimately commune with the Father can we bless a needy world.

Try It Yourself

Deepen conversational prayer with Abba.

Read John 17 if you've not done so already. Notice that in this lengthy prayer of Jesus, only half a dozen verses contain a petition or request.

In your prayer time, consciously strive to supplement petitionary prayer with "conversational engagement"[2] that involves opening your heart to the Lord, acknowledging His goodness, giving Him praise, and sharing with Him your deepest hopes and dreams.

Do you find that your relationship with the Father has deepened as a result of practicing intimate conversation?

Deepening Surrender

FOLLOWING HIS FAREWELL PRAYER, JESUS LED HIS ANXIOUS FOLLOWERS TO the Garden of Gethsemane, at the base of the Mount of Olives. Gethsemane—meaning "oil press"—was the place where olives were crushed to produce oil. Perhaps a wealthy friend provided this quiet site where Jesus and the disciples frequently retired for prayer. Jesus told eight disciples to wait near the entrance of the olive grove while He led the inner circle (Peter, James, and John) a few paces into the garden. As we reflect on what occurred there, we enter sacred space. We recall God's words to Moses centuries earlier: "Take off your sandals, for the place where you are standing is holy ground" (Exodus 3:5).

Distress

Matthew 26:36-45; Mark 14:32-39; Luke 22:39-46

As Jesus fell to His knees in prayer, Matthew tells us that He "began to be sorrowful and troubled" (Matthew 26:37). The first word *(lupeō)* means "sad" or "distressed." The second *(adēmoneō)* literally means "away from home" or "decentered." Mark, in even stronger language, states that Jesus "began to be deeply distressed and troubled" (Mark 14:33). Mark's additional descriptor, "deeply distressed" (or *ekthambeomai*), means "overcome with amazement and terror." As *The Message* puts it (Mark 14:33), Jesus "plunged into a sinkhole of dreadful agony." Jesus was agitated, disoriented, and bewildered at what lay before Him.

In agony, Jesus said to the three disciples, "My soul is overwhelmed with sorrow to the point of death" (Matthew 26:38). The Gospels present the Son of God in the garden as a vulnerable human, not a valiant hero. As William Lane noted, "Jesus came [to Gethsemane] to be with the Father for an interlude before his betrayal, but found hell rather than heaven opened before him, and he staggered."[1] Anticipating the Cross, the Son of Man experienced severe emotional distress. We find him craving human sympathy—longing to share His sorrow with intimate friends.

Jesus then said to Peter, James, and John, "Stay here and keep watch with me" (Matthew 26:38). Tearing Himself from His friends, Jesus entered the shadows of the olive trees alone. There the Son prayed to the Father as no other person ever prayed.

Bargaining

IN THE FIRST of His three prayers Jesus said, "Papa, Father, you can — can't you? — get me out of this. Take this cup away from me" (Mark 14:36, MSG). The Aramaic-Greek phrase *Abba* — "Papa, Father" — expresses the most intimate relationship. The Son cried out to His beloved Father as a distressed child cries out to his earthly daddy. The cup Jesus prayed to escape symbolizes God's wrath meted out against sin, and His own blood poured out as an atonement.

In this first prayer, Jesus as man recoiled from the horror of what confronted Him: betrayal by a chosen friend, intense conflict with Satan, the physical pain of the cross. Worst of all He faced the spiritual desolation of abandonment by the Father, reflected in His prayer on the cross: "My God, my God, why have you forsaken me?" (Mark 15:34). In this first prayer, Jesus, as it were, asked if there was any other way God's kingdom might be realized than through the pain and anguish of death. Dale Bruner comments: "All that the text allows us to know is that, if possible, Jesus wanted out, and we are asked to honor the mystery of that request."[2] The author of Hebrews agreed: Jesus "offered up prayers and petitions with loud cries and tears to the one who could *save him from death*" (5:7, emphasis added).

As Jesus staggered under the weight of the struggle, an angel ministered strength and encouragement — as following His temptation in the wilderness (see Matthew 4:11). Yet so intense was His anguish in prayer that in the cool night, sweat poured from His body like blood oozing from a wound. Returning to the garden gate, Jesus found the three disciples sleeping, emotionally drained from the uncertainty and stress.

Acceptance

JESUS RETIRED INTO the garden and prayed a second time: "My Father, if there is no other way than this, drinking this cup to the dregs, I'm ready. Do it your way" (Matthew 26:42, MSG). The Lord's second prayer reveals growing acceptance of the Father's will. In His first prayer Jesus had prayed for a less painful path, but the Father in wisdom answered with a loving "No."

Fortified by communion with His Father in prayer, Jesus no longer asked that the cup of suffering be removed. Once again He returned to check on the disciples, only to find them sound asleep. "Could you men not keep watch with me for one hour?" He asked (Matthew 26:40).

Jesus' third prayer was one of complete acceptance of the path of suffering. In spite of the indescribable physical, emotional, and spiritual pain He would experience, Jesus fully embraced the path appointed by the Father.

Why did Jesus in Gethsemane pray a second and a third time? Elijah prayed three times for a widow's son to be healed (see 1 Kings 17:21), and Paul prayed three times for a thorn in the flesh to be removed (see 2 Corinthians 12:8). Jesus' repeated prayers reflect urgency and persistence in His hour of temptation. But more than this, Jesus' wrestling in prayer reflects a struggle within His own soul. That Satan was tempting Jesus to turn back from the Cross is a part of this. But Jesus as man anticipated the agony of taking upon Himself the sin and guilt of the entire world—or as Paul later put it, of being made sin for us (see 2 Corinthians 5:21).

Peace

It seems that Jesus' struggle in prayer reflects the stages of grief we humans experience: the shock of disbelief, anger, bargaining, and finally, acceptance and peace.

As Jesus prayed and drew wisdom from the Father, His will became progressively more aligned with the Father's will. In His Gethsemane prayers, Jesus moved from a ten o'clock to an eleven o'clock to a twelve o'clock position with respect to God's will.[3] Jesus' entire life was a continual process of submission to the Father's will. At no time was this more evident than in the Garden of Gethsemane.

Jesus prayed repeatedly because He needed to take in the love, encouragement, and strength that would enable Him to obey the Father's will. He desired to do what His Father wanted, but He needed the enablement to do it. It was necessary for the Son to draw from the Father resources sufficient for the grave challenges ahead. As the author of Hebrews states, "Having been made *perfect*, he became the source of eternal salvation for all who obey him" (5:9, NRSV, emphasis added).

Returning a third time to the disciples, Jesus found them once again asleep, perhaps in a state of stupor. Lane notes, "The greater the stress of the approaching passion, the more selfish and confused those around him became."[4] Jesus woke the disciples and, seeing Judas and the mob approaching, said, "Rise, let us go!" (Matthew 26:46). His spirit fortified and His vision clarified through communion with the Father and the angelic visitation, Jesus set His face to Calvary with calm confidence.

This Gethsemane account tells us that Jesus, as Son of Man, couldn't manage the challenge of the Cross on His own. To do the Father's will, He needed to draw nourishment, strength, and direction sufficient for the task.

If Jesus, God's Son, needed nurture from the Father, how much more then do we human ministers who follow in His train? For indeed, "the spirit is willing, but the body is weak" (Mark 14:38).

Try It Yourself

Align your will with the Father's will.

Identify a life issue that you're presently struggling with. It may be a difficult decision needing to be made, an illness, or a major redirecting of your life.

Prayerfully ponder the extent to which self will is involved in this struggle.

Guided by Jesus' experience in Gethsemane, what would it take for you to surrender this matter fully to God and accept His wise and perfect will?

Leaping into Abba's Arms

AFTER BEING NAILED TO A CROSS BETWEEN TWO THIEVES, JESUS HUNG there in excruciating pain for six hours—beginning at about 9 in the morning. But this would be no ordinary day.

From noon to 3 P.M.—the brightest part of the day—the sun stopped shining and darkness shrouded the land. This was not a solar eclipse, for Passover was celebrated at full moon, when the sun and moon were at opposite poles of the earth. The darkness that occurred reflects nature mourning over this most heinous crime. Darkness is also a symbol of Satan's activity. As Jesus hung on the cross, the light of the world was temporarily extinguished.

In that dark hour, death reigned. Satan appeared to have triumphed. The earthquake and the breaking open of the tombs testified that nature itself was in pain, convulsing at the death of God's Son. "Nature itself rebelled," as it were, "against what men were doing to nature's God."[1]

At 3 P.M., when the daily lamb would be sacrificed in the temple, Jesus cried out with a loud voice, "My God, my God, why have you abandoned me?" (Matthew 27:46, MSG). This was Jesus' fourth utterance from the cross, quoting Psalm 22:1. The "me" is emphatic. It was as if Jesus said, "I am your beloved Son and servant who has kept your word. Why *me?*"

What caused Jesus to utter this cry of dereliction? In that moment Jesus symbolically drank the bitter cup containing the world's sin and guilt. As Isaiah predicted, "Surely he took up our infirmities and carried our sorrows, yet we considered him stricken by God, smitten by him, and afflicted" (Isaiah 53:4). In that brief moment the punishment of human sin was heaped on Jesus' blameless body and soul, and He cried out in pain.

Furthermore, Jesus cried out because God the Father temporarily abandoned God the Son. The word *abandon* that fell from Jesus' lips means to "leave in the lurch" or to "provide no help." For a brief space the Son's communion with the Father was severed, His vision of the Father clouded—not because of some interpersonal conflict between Himself and the Father, but because the Father could not look upon the Lamb bearing the world's sin.

In this moment, Jesus exclaimed, not "My Father," but "My God"— the only time He used this address. How God the Father could abandon God the Son, even for a moment, is a mystery we will never understand this side of glory. But to be separated from God however briefly—that is darkness; that is torture. That is hell.

Notice that Jesus died asking the question, "*Why?*"

"Why am I abandoned by the God I love, trust, and serve?" It's significant that during His earthly sojourn Jesus asked our kind of questions. The Father didn't reply to Jesus' profound question with words; He would do so shortly with Resurrection power. Yet in spite of the unanswered question, Jesus never lost faith in the Father, for His cry was, "*My* God." Jesus trusted God the Father, even when for a brief space God was not there for Him.

So horrible was this scene that the onlookers beat their breasts out of shock that a righteous man should so suffer—perhaps also out of self-condemnation that they had been party to the crucifixion of an innocent man (see Luke 23:47-48).

Jesus' Consolation

Matthew 27:45-50; Mark 15:33-37; Luke 23:44-46; John 19:28-30

Parched, exhausted, and in deep pain, Jesus cried out for a drink. Bystanders lifted a sponge dipped in vinegar to His lips. Hanging onto life by a thread, Jesus said, "It is finished" (John 19:30).

With redemption's provision completed, the Son "called out with a loud voice, 'Father, into your hands I commit my spirit'" (Luke 23:46). This was His seventh and last cry from the cross, quoting Psalm 31:5. The "loud voice," uttered with His last burst of energy as life was slipping away, was an expression of deep conviction and firm confidence. The Father honored His Son's sacrifice. Fellowship was restored; atonement for sin was made. Jesus once again was able to address God with the intimate, family name "Father."

We can understand why an innocent man inflicted with such torture might be filled with bitterness and anger. But though He was wracked with indescribable pain and assaulted by dark powers, Jesus never gave up on His Father. Surrounded by deep gloom, He kept clinging to the Father in faith and love. As His life was being extinguished, Jesus leapt into His Father's nurturing arms to receive the ultimate spiritual direction: the eternal embrace of compassionate Abba.

Luke reports that Jesus "breathed his last" (Luke 23:46). Matthew's description, "he gave up (literally 'sent away') his spirit" (27:50), indicates that Jesus voluntarily surrendered His life unto death. Witnessing the manner of Jesus' demise, a Roman centurion confessed what the Jewish religious leaders denied—that the Crucified One was "a righteous man" (Luke 23:47). Indeed, He was . . . and is . . . "the Son of God" (Mark 15:39).

What a great image this spiritual warfare of Jesus on the cross provides for every one of us who needs soul care. In the worst hours of our lives, when our souls are wracked with hellish pain and we feel that even God has abandoned us, Jesus is our example.

Like Him, we can direct our souls to "leap" by faith into the Father's arms. And there, we will experience the fellowship and care of our great Abba.

Abba is there for His children — always and forever!

TRY IT YOURSELF

Is Jesus your ultimate refuge?

Perhaps in your Christian walk you have fallen into a pit of discouragement, where you feel let down or even abandoned by God.

Record in your journal the questions you would ask God amidst your confusion and anguish.

Are you willing by faith to leap into Abba's arms and receive the love and consolation He offers you as His blood-bought child?

PART 4

GUIDING OTHERS, JESUS-STYLE

After the Pattern of Jesus

Part 1 of this book presented Jesus and His ministry as the
Christian disciple's model for soul care, or spiritual direction. Part 2
examined encounters recorded in Scripture in which Jesus ministered spiritual guidance to family, friends, strangers, and adversaries. Virtually every
conversation Jesus had and every teaching He gave imparted spiritual guidance, because He was constantly pointing people toward God. Part 3
explored how Jesus drew nourishment for His own soul from His heavenly
Father.

In this last part, we summarize Jesus' style of spiritual direction and the
qualities He brought to the sacred task. The Lord was remarkably flexible
in ministering to people in their searches for meaningful relationship with
God. He offered no simplistic answers and no neat formulas for spiritual
growth. Yet we find in His ministry a pattern that can inform disciples who
minister spiritual guidance today.

Jesus' Approach to Spiritual Guidance

Jesus made Himself available to people.
The Master, whose mission was "to serve, and to give his life as a ransom
for many" (Mark 10:45), was openly accessible to people of every social,
economic, and political stripe—to rich and poor, religious and sinners,
politicians and peasants, Jews and Gentiles.

For those of us with busy lives and many demands upon us, we need
to recognize that Jesus allowed His "schedule" to be interrupted by people
with urgent longings and pressing needs. When a Roman centurion peti-
tioned Jesus to heal his sick servant, Jesus replied, "I will go and heal him"
(Matthew 8:7). On another occasion, Jesus halted a procession headed to
Jerusalem to heal two blind men (Matthew 20:30-34). Jesus was the most
other-centered person who ever lived.

Jesus ministered in the power of the Spirit.
The Spirit of God came upon Jesus at His baptism (see Mark 1:9-11),
mightily anointing Him for public ministry. The Holy Spirit—the personal presence and power of God—is the principal spiritual director. Jesus

was led and empowered by that holy presence as He ministered spiritual guidance to souls seeking relationship with God and purpose in life.

Jesus dealt with persons as unique individuals.

Jesus honored each person's uniqueness as image of God. He didn't prescribe one rule for everybody. He ministered uniquely to this person, in this situation, with this need, and at this time in her life. He told the man from whom the demon was cast out to return to his family (see Mark 5:18-20), whereas to another man he said, "Come, follow me" (Mark 10:21). Even when speaking to a large crowd, Jesus addressed each one personally: "He who has ears, let him hear" (Matthew 13:9,43).

Jesus engaged people in creative dialogue.

Jesus' teaching, itself a form of spiritual guidance, often gave way to dialogue or lively verbal interchanges. The Lord gave people opportunities to unburden their hearts and tell their stories. To possess one's soul in peace, one must disclose his soul. Dialogue with Jesus stripped away illusions and led to a deeper seeing, hearing, and understanding. Jesus mirrored thoughts, feelings, and aspirations, such that people saw themselves and their need for God more clearly. He didn't allow dialogue to deteriorate into fruitless debate, as, for example, when He dialogued with the Samaritan woman at the well.

Through creative dialogue with Jesus, people were challenged to constructive change.

Jesus asked probing questions.

Unlike Socrates's questions, which were crafted to stimulate intellectual understanding, Jesus' questions prodded people to examine their hearts and God's claim on their lives. In conversation, Jesus often led or countered with a probing question crafted to stimulate self-examination (see John 1:38), thoughtful reflection about spiritual issues (see Luke 18:40-41), and clarification of motives (see John 5:6; Acts 9:4). By penetrating interrogations Jesus unmasked illusions (see John 13:38), focused on core issues of human destiny (see Matthew 9:4-5), and called for decision (see John 18:34). Jesus' questions, in short, invited hearers to journey inward in pursuit of the kingdom of God. His questioning illustrates the nondirective aspect of spiritual guidance.

Jesus listened attentively and empathetically.

Jesus first of all listened to the Father to hear His word and discern His will (see John 8:28). Ministering to others, He practiced "active listening," focusing undivided attention on the person before Him so as to enter into her experience. He listened to people's expressions of fear, frustration, failure, and seeds of faith. Listening with heart as well as ears, Jesus heard the pain and aspirations embedded in the spoken words. Often Jesus would say nothing, creating pauses, or silent spaces, in which the still, small voice of God might be heard. When a Canaanite woman told Jesus about her demon-possessed daughter, "Jesus did not answer a word" (Matthew 15:23), His silence allowing space for reflection and decision. Because people often can be helped by our listening rather than talking, "the first service that one owes to others . . . consists in listening to them."[1] Listening well—at least to the end of a sentence—further illustrates the nondirective side of spiritual guidance.

Jesus skillfully applied the Word of God to people's lives.

Jesus taught the Word of God to seekers, stressing themes of sin, repentance, forgiveness, and kingdom living. His thorough knowledge of the Old Testament (the Bible of His day) enabled Him to apply its teachings relevantly to people's needs. He interpreted the Commandments to the rich young man (see Mark 10:19-21) and expounded the Scriptures to Cleopas and another disciple (see Luke 24:27). As A. W. Tozer observed, "The Word of God well understood and religiously obeyed is the shortest route to spiritual perfection."[2]

Jesus affirmed and encouraged people on their faith journeys.

Human beings have a fundamental need for affirmation of worth. Lacking this, we become discouraged and give up. Actress Celeste Holm rightly said, "We live by encouragement and we die without it, slowly, sadly, and angrily." Jesus' affirmation and encouragement lifted people to higher ground spiritually. Jesus encouraged Peter following his denials by entrusting him with the feeding and care of the flock (see John 21:15-18).

Jesus identified obstacles to spiritual growth.

With disarming directness, Jesus unmasked illusions and identified impediments to relationship with the triune God. He singled out distorted images of the Father, unhealthy fears, avoidance techniques, and sinful behavior patterns that cloud relationship. Jesus knew that sinful passions such as pride, anger, fear, and an unforgiving spirit close a person's heart to grace. So also do excessive busyness, guilt, and self-loathing. Jesus told the rich young man that love of possessions blocked his access to the kingdom (see Luke 18:22-25). Identifying obstacles to growth illustrates the directive side of spiritual guidance.

Jesus challenged, confronted, corrected, and rebuked.

After earning the right to be heard, Jesus told persons the truth about life and themselves (see Luke 9:58,62). Many times Jesus said to hearers, "I tell you the truth" (Matthew 5:18; 8:10; 16:28). The Lord never soft-pedaled the truth to curry people's favor. He challenged people to take responsibility for their lives and live out the demands of the gospel. He confronted friends with their laziness and dullness of heart and adversaries with their hard-heartedness. His rebuke was gentle in the case of His mother at Cana (see John 2:4) and the two disciples on the road to Emmaus (see Luke 24:25-26). It was firm in the case of James and John (see Luke 9:54) and Peter (see Matthew 16:23). Jesus didn't hesitate to disturb people's false sense of peace. When telling people what they must do, He never coerced or manipulated them against their wills. Here again is a directive aspect of spiritual guidance.

Jesus patiently bore with people's ignorance, pride, laziness, and failures.

Confident of what people might become by grace, Jesus "hung in there" with His disciples, never giving up on them. Jesus forgave the disciples when they failed to watch with Him in the Garden (see Matthew 26:40,43,45) and when they fled following His arrest (see Matthew 26:56). He gave erring followers the hope that no sin is too great for God to forgive. Jesus never condemned nor shamed a person; but neither did He permit people to offer lame excuses for their behavior.

Jesus was fervent in prayer for those to whom He ministered.

Jesus prayed for His disciples and the unbelieving world when alone with God in solitary places. He prayed for their needs and for their release into God's loving arms. He prayed with His disciples in the Upper Room for their growth in purity, unity, and protection from the evil one (see John 17:6-19). Jesus' life was an unfinished symphony of prayer for others. According to Gerald May, "Spiritual guidance does not have to be passive or solemn, but it should be prayerful and reverent."[3]

Jesus ministered soul care in community.

Jesus' primary ministry was guiding the twelve disciples. Following the Resurrection, Jesus ministered peace and encouragement "when the disciples were together" (John 20:19). When ministering to outsiders, Jesus surrounded Himself with His disciple friends. The Lord sought to build community, knowing that community is the context in which the Spirit evokes new life. Soul care is most effectively ministered through the supportive circle of the believing community.

Jesus experienced resistance in giving spiritual direction.
Jesus longed to lead people to deeper faith and obedience. He earnestly invited people to the living water, but honoring human freedom, did not compel them to drink. Thus, after dialoguing with Jesus, the rich young ruler left sad and empty. After accompanying Jesus for three years, Judas betrayed the Lord for thirty silver coins. Spiritual directors will pray and plead, but the outcome will not always be as they desire.

Jesus ministered with a sense of lightheartedness.
Although dealing with issues of eternal destiny, Jesus celebrated life on the lighter side by attending a party in Cana where He rejoiced with the bride and groom. Jesus evidenced in His ministry a childlike playfulness and a ready sense of humor. He knew the value of unstructured leisure. The Lord didn't allow His ministry of soul care to turn into a "gigantic heavy."[4]

Jesus cared for His own soul.
Jesus knew His physical and emotional limits as Son of Man. He took time for rest, recreation, and social relationships. The Son of God knew that He must faithfully nourish intimacy with the Father if He would reflect Him well to weary pilgrims. Thus, throughout His ministry Jesus sought and received spiritual nurture from His loving Father. He regularly withdrew from the crowds (see Mark 3:7-9) for seasons of solitude (see Mark 6:32), prayer for personal needs, and nourishing communion with Abba (see Luke 6:12). By regularly taking in spiritual nourishment, Jesus "never allowed his own needs to get in the way of meeting the needs of others."[5]

Jesus showed that the spiritual director's task is to listen, question, suggest, encourage, correct, offer resources, and pray with and for disciples. The spiritual care-giver serves in Jesus' name by prayerfully following the pattern set forth by the Master.

TRY IT YOURSELF
Give yourself a ministry checkup.
As you minister spiritual guidance — informally or formally, in your parish or other setting — prayerfully seek to follow the pattern Jesus established, as outlined in this chapter.

Which ministry practices of Jesus do you find most difficult for you to emulate?

Process these issues, whether they be listening empathetically or caring for your own soul, with an experienced spiritual director.

After the Character of Jesus

MONICA HAD BEEN SEEKING SPIRITUAL GUIDANCE AND DIRECTION FOR a long time. So had Chuck. At the outset, neither one had had good experiences.

Monica thought she'd found a godly man to offer direction and insight. For several years they'd met about once every three months, during which time Monica would seek his guidance on how to walk more closely with God in obedience to the Christian service she felt called to—which was teaching Scripture to younger women in her church.

One day, however, Monica became very aware that this man wanted more than a spiritual relationship—even though both of them were married. When she confronted him, he admitted that he had "a problem" with counseling women, which had sometimes gotten him into trouble. Of course, their relationship as spiritual director and directee ended that day, but not before the man promised to step out of his role as director for a time to seek professional and spiritual help.

Chuck's relationship with a spiritual director started out similarly. He was amazed and grateful for the depth of spiritual insight his director showed, and for the way his counsel and encouragement made it possible for Chuck to walk in greater closeness and obedience to God.

But in time, Chuck noticed something change. At first he couldn't put his finger on it—and then it became clear. The guidance he was receiving was no longer coming from Scripture, or from scriptural principles; it was coming from the works of popular authors you might see on daytime TV talk shows. When he raised this issue with his director, the man shrugged it off. Chuck believed that, in a way, all truth is God's truth. But he needed to know he was being directed from a sound, scriptural foundation—not from pop or new-age psychology.

Both Monica and Chuck moved on to find new spiritual directors. Both recognized that human beings are flawed and changeable, and they didn't allow themselves to become disheartened about their experiences. Despite their disappointments, they continued to keep soul care as a high priority.

While we need to remember that human beings are, after all, "only human," it's very important that we experience, or offer, safety in our spiritually directive relationships. Because we are talking about a relationship in which one party is opening himself or herself at the deepest levels, the relationship must be founded in godliness and trust.

What are qualities we need to look for, or to offer, in a spiritually directive relationship?

Jesus, Our Perfect Model

During His earthly ministry Jesus exuded qualities that made Him the director of souls *par excellence*. Here are some of the more important character qualities Jesus possessed.

He had a thorough knowledge of the Scriptures and other disciplines.
Jesus' knowledge of the Old Testament was perfect, such that He could quote it accurately and apply it wisely to people's needs. Jesus illumined the life experiences of His hearers by citing examples of biblical characters with needs similar to their own. He also had a deep knowledge of theology, human nature, and spiritual warfare. In addition, the Lord possessed profound self-knowledge—conscious of His identity as Son of God and Son of Man.

To be effective, spiritual directors should be well-grounded in the Bible, theology, the spiritual classics, and principles of human behavior. Teresa of Avila (d. 1582) wrote, "It is best to consult one both spiritual and learned."[1]

He had a deep experience of the spiritual life.
Jesus enjoyed an intimate relationship with Abba, His joy and strength. He delighted in deep communion with His heavenly Father. Said He, "No one knows the Son except the Father, and no one knows the Father except the Son" (Matthew 11:27). Jesus' intimate relationship with the Father fortified Him for the pressures and challenges of public ministry. Living in the Father's presence and listening to His voice enabled Jesus to reveal Him to seeking souls. The contemporary spiritual guide will make pursuit of God an absolute priority, for one cannot give away what one does not possess.

He cultivated a prayerful spirit.
Prayer was the lifeblood of Jesus' ministry. He regularly retired to solitary and quiet places to seek the Father's face in prayer. The Lord communed with Abba on ordinary, uneventful days as well as on occasions of special significance and challenge, such as at His baptism (see Luke 3:21), before calling the twelve disciples (see Luke 6:12), at His Transfiguration (see Luke 9:28), in the Upper Room (see John 17), and in Gethsemane (see Matthew 26:36-43). By receiving the touch of God's invisible presence in prayer, Jesus appropriated the wisdom, strength, and direction needed to fulfill His mission.

Men and women who minister soul care will cultivate a vibrant prayer life, without which, spiritual life withers and dies.

He had loving concern for others.
Jesus' heart abounded with love for all and compassion for those in distress. When the Lord saw the widow from Nain grieving over her dead son, "His heart went out to her" (Luke 7:13). Later He wept with Mary and Martha over the death of Lazarus (see John 11:33-36). Jesus' love and compassion served as a conduit through which God's grace flowed to others. His loving words and actions gave hearers the confidence to commit their lives to Him. As the Taizé chant puts it, "Where there is kindness and love, there God is."[2]

Jesus also abounded in empathy—the capacity to enter the individual worlds of others and to experience life from their perspectives. Spiritual mentors discover that love, compassion, and empathy are more valuable commodities than therapeutic expertise.

He had the gift of discernment.
Discernment is the "charism," or Spirit-gift, by which one intuits thoughts (see Luke 5:22), reads motives (see John 6:61), and distinguishes true from false spirits (see 1 Corinthians 12:10). In the Bible that Jesus knew, discernment was a prized quality: "The mocker seeks wisdom and finds none, but knowledge comes easily to the discerning" (Proverbs 14:6). During His ministry Jesus discerned the wiles of the devil in the wilderness (see Matthew 4:3-12), understood peoples' hearts better than they knew themselves (see Luke 7:40; 9:48), and perceived the Father's will (see Matthew 26:39-44).

Spiritual guides will pray for and cultivate the biblical gift of discernment (see Hebrews 5:14). As John Cassian (d. 435) somewhere wrote, "Become money-changers, able to distinguish gold from brass and to accept only genuine coin."

He practiced holiness of life.
Jesus' character and conduct were marked by unswerving holiness and truth. A follower who observed Him closely concluded that Jesus was "the Holy and Righteous One" (Acts 3:14). Graced with uprightness and integrity, Jesus was qualified to lead others into God's holy presence. When asked to identify the quality most important in a spiritual care-giver, seminarians ranked holiness of life highest.[3] Following Jesus, spiritual mentors will "[m]ake every effort . . . to be holy; without holiness no one will see the Lord" (Hebrews 12:14).

He had a peaceful heart.

Jesus' soul was at peace because He was comfortably "at home" with Himself and with His Father. From this reservoir of peace He was fully present to troubled pilgrims. Free from anxiety and stress, Jesus offered hospitable sanctuary to restless souls. Following the Resurrection, Jesus bequeathed this same peace to His servants: "Peace be with you" (John 20:19,21,26). Patience flowed from His peaceful condition. Never in a hurry, Jesus patiently waited for God's perfect timing.

He knew well the experience of suffering.

Jesus lived a life of suffering. He was misunderstood by His half-brothers, rejected by the masses, hated by the religious authorities, and consigned to an excruciating death. Because Jesus suffered physically, emotionally, and spiritually, "He is able to deal gently with those who are ignorant and are going astray, since he himself is subject to weakness" (Hebrews 5:2).

A person who has experienced only the comforts of salvation ("consolations") and not brokenness and rejection ("desolations") finds it more difficult to empathize with those undergoing trials. But one who has experienced and dealt redemptively with doubts and disappointments can more competently minister to those experiencing such trials (see 2 Corinthians 1:3-6).

The effective spiritual director, according to Henri Nouwen, is a "wounded healer"[4]—a saint broken, but marvelously restored and renewed.

He developed a sense of wonder.

Jesus' heart was filled with a profound sense of the grandeur of God. In His High Priestly Prayer, Jesus said to the Father, "I have given them the glory that you gave me" (John 17:22). Exuding a deep sense of the divine in its majesty and mystery, Jesus welcomed seeking souls into God's spacious presence.

Prayerful imitation of these and other qualities possessed in perfection by our Lord will ensure that our ministry of spiritual guidance will bear much fruit. The virtues Jesus modeled may be cultivated through prayer, study, and faithful practice.

We who mentor or guide others on the sacred path must pray for wisdom sufficient for this high calling. We must also be prepared to work faithfully at this sacred task.

Reginald Somerset Ward (d. 1962), a leading Anglican spiritual director, somewhere summed up the essential qualities of an effective spiritual guide, or director, this way:

> One pound of spiritual direction is made up of eight ounces
>   of prayer,

three ounces of theology, three ounces of common sense, and two ounces of psychology.

TRY IT YOURSELF

Give yourself a character checkup.

Reflect on those qualities Jesus possessed that made Him the model spiritual director.

For each of the qualities cited in this chapter, rate your competency as "excellent," "good," or "needing improvement."

Prayerfully devise a plan that will foster growth in the areas of need you have identified—such as spiritual discernment or holiness of life.

Epilogue

WE HAVE EXAMINED THE LIFE-GIVING, BUT NEGLECTED, MINISTRY OF soul care—or spiritual direction. We have found that Jesus, in the power of the Spirit, ministered spiritual guidance to both men and women, the rich and poor, the educated and uneducated of His day.

Who Needs Spiritual Direction Today?

WHETHER YOUNG OR old, a lay person, pastor, missionary, or seminarian, all journeying Christians will profit from the ministry of spiritual guidance as explained in this book. All who hunger to know God more intimately, to pray more passionately, to discern God's will more clearly, to navigate life's pathway more successfully will find a rich bounty in the ministry of spiritual guidance. If you sincerely desire to grow in the "grace and knowledge of our Lord and Savior Jesus Christ" (2 Peter 3:18), spiritual guidance is for you!

Where to Go for Spiritual Direction

WHERE CAN A disciple who is eager to grow spiritually find a person who will listen, discern, keep his feet to the fire, and point the way home? Where can one find a supportive spiritual companion endued with wisdom, compassion, humility, and grace? Advice givers and problem solvers are as common as coal in Newcastle. But where are the godly and competent spiritual guides—those who to a significant degree reflect the pastoral qualities exhibited by the Lord Jesus?

There may be a shred of truth in the opinion that "Good spiritual directors are as rare as hen's teeth."[1] The fact is, however, that God has graced His church with competent spiritual directors who would consider it a privilege to help nurture your growth in Christ.

A good place to begin is to seek a referral from your pastor, minister of congregational care, or a lay care-giver. It may be helpful to inquire at a nearby cathedral, retreat center, denominational office, or a college or seminary that offers a program in spiritual direction. Speak to a person who has, or is, meeting with a competent spiritual director. It may prove useful to consult the Web site of the professional organization Spiritual Directors International.[2]

Most importantly, ask God to lead you to the person ideally suited to your temperament and needs. You may be surprised how marvelously God will send the right servant your way. He who persistently seeks, finds. Teresa of Avila, whose life was richly graced by the ministry of spiritual direction, noted, "The Lord will give you a director if you are really humble, and desire to meet with the right person."[3]

How to Prepare to Be a Spiritual Director

WHETHER YOU WISH to serve informally as a spiritual friend or more formally as a spiritual director, every additional measure of training you obtain will make you a more effective tool in God's hand. The current revival of interest in the ministry of Christian spiritual direction, especially within the evangelical community, means that a growing number of opportunities exist whereby you may be schooled in this helping art.

The following is a short list of effective training programs in spiritual guidance or direction:

Denver Seminary
Program in Evangelical Spiritual Guidance (held in Denver and
    Colorado Springs, Colorado)
Box 100,000
Denver, CO 80250
www.denverseminary.edu

Talbot School of Theology
The Institute for Spiritual Formation
13800 Biola Avenue
La Mirada, CA 90639
www.talbot.edu

Christos Center for Spiritual Formation
1212 Holly Lane
Lino Lakes, MN 55038
www.christoscenter.org

Epiphany Association
947 Tropical Avenue
Pittsburgh, PA 15216
www.epiphanyassociation.org

School for Charismatic Spiritual Directors
Pecos Benedictine Abbey
Box 1080
Pecos, NM 87552
www.pecosabbey.org
("Charismatic" indicates that spiritual direction is a charism, or
enablement, of the Holy Spirit.)
The Website of Spiritual Directors International
(http://www.sdiworld.org) contains a full listing of spiritual direction
training programs (many ecumenical) by states of the union.

In closing, I pray that you experience fruitful journeying in a spiritual
direction that takes you ever closer to God!

Historical Journey Patterns

EARLY IN THIS BOOK, BRIEF MENTION WAS MADE OF THE DIFFERENT "patterns" earlier Christians have written about in an effort to describe the soul's journey to greater intimacy with God. We looked at a contemporary model, but in fact many different models exist.

Of these, perhaps the most famous are those described by Bernard of Clairvaux, Teresa of Avila, and the Puritan John Bunyan. Those models are described here in brief: first, to give you an understanding of their design, and also to help you see if you, or someone under your soul care, might identify with one or more of these patterns. Using them as a general "map" for spiritual direction may prove helpful—though we must always remember that God Himself is the director of souls, and every soul's journey will be unique.

The Medieval Model: Intensifying Love

BERNARD OF CLAIRVAUX (d. 1153), who wrote such cherished hymns as "Jesus, the Very Thought of Thee," "O Sacred Head Now Wounded," and "Jesus, Thou Joy of Loving Hearts," described the spiritual journey as the increase of love in four degrees. Spiritual growth involves the deepening experience of love.[1]

"We love ourselves for our own sake."

This, according to Bernard, is the first degree of love. The law is summed up in the command, "Love your neighbor as yourself" (Leviticus 19:18; Matthew 22:39). As the proverb puts it, "To acquire wisdom is to love oneself" (Proverbs 19:8, NLT). It's a sound psychological principle that a person cannot love God or others until she first loves herself as a valued creation. This first degree of love is *immature love,* or "love of self for self."

"We love God for our own sake."

In this degree, young Christians love God for the benefits He bestows, such as answering prayers and supplying needs. This is *immature love,* or "love of self for self."

"We love God for God's sake."

Here, the medieval saint says, the expanding heart yearns for the Giver behind the gifts, the God of consolations more than the consolations of God. Through deepening communion with the altogether Lovely One (see Song of Songs, 5:16), the soul seeks no other reward than God Himself. This is *unselfish love,* or "love of God for self."

"We love ourselves for God's sake."

Bernard describes the fourth degree, where, loving God with a pure love, we know experientially God's unfathomable love for us. This is *perfect love,* or "love of self for God." The Puritan Richard Sibbes described the journey of deepening of love in similar terms: "A Christian begins with loving God for himself. But he ends in loving himself in and for God. And so, his end and God's end . . . agree in one."[2]

The Carmelite Model: Deepening Prayer

TERESA OF AVILA (d. 1582) in *The Interior Castle* portrayed the spiritual journey as a deepening relationship with God through prayer. The castle represents the human soul, the gate of the castle entry into the spiritual life, and the innermost room of the castle the place of deepest communion with God. Teresa compares the pilgrim's passage through the castle to the relationship between a lover and the beloved—progressing from spiritual friendship (rooms 1-3), to spiritual courtship (rooms 4-5), to spiritual marriage (rooms 6-7).

Spiritual Friendship

The new convert entering the first dwelling place has had an encounter with God, but has not yet developed a relationship with Him. The soul is torn between the attractions of the world and the things of God. "In the first room souls are still absorbed in the world and engulfed in their pleasures and vanities."[3]

In the second dwelling place, the convert's faith remains feeble, prayers brief and lukewarm, and service self-centered. Satan attacks the Christian by recalling his need for financial security and worldly acclaim. Considerable tension exists at the level of inner values; the Christian's soul is torn between going forward with Christ and returning to the world.

In the third dwelling place, growth continues through sermons, books, and friendships. While outwardly performing acts of charity, inwardly the person lacks intimacy with Christ. In the third room, many souls experience spiritual dryness or a dark night of the soul. God permits such trials in order to increase dependency on Him. Many Christians, discouraged by their desolations, fail to progress beyond this third stage.

Spiritual Courtship

In the fourth dwelling place the journeyer, exercised by her trials, engages God more profoundly. By allowing the Spirit to draw the faculties inward through the prayer of quiet, the Christian deepens intimacy with the Savior. The heart now becomes the channel for receiving grace. Teresa likens this to a courting couple who relate to each other through the heart's secret affections. In this stage the Christian's focus is love, not rules.

Teresa judged that relatively few Christians reach the fifth dwelling place. The soul that journeys here becomes so centered that a profound experience of communion with Christ in prayer occurs. Teresa compared the soul's transformation in Christ to that of a silkworm, which builds a cocoon, is transformed within its tent, and emerges as a beautiful butterfly. In this room the soul is so attracted to Christ that it longs to leave the world and be with Him. Still the heart has not found its perfect resting place.

Spiritual Marriage

Those who enter the sixth dwelling place discover that love for the Bridegroom intensifies beyond words. So clear is the sense of God's presence that the Christian experiences raptures and visions of Christ, not unlike Moses' experience at the burning bush (see Exodus 3:2-6). In this stage the Christian may suffer physical afflictions or persecutions, which are but wounds of love. "All these sufferings are meant to increase one's desire to enjoy the Spouse."[4] The pilgrim at this stage becomes a prophetic voice for the community.

Finally, in the seventh dwelling place the soul is brought into closest possible union with Christ this side of glory. Fleeting moments of rapture are elevated into more sustained communion with the Beloved. Christ has become married to all aspects of the conscious and unconscious mind, such that the Christian thinks, wills, and acts with the mind of Christ. In this stage the beloved becomes a willing slave of Christ and a compassionate servant of the needy. "What God communicates here to the soul is a secret so great and a favor so sublime . . . that I don't know what to compare it to. I can only say that the Lord wishes to reveal for that moment, in a more sublime manner than any spiritual vision or taste, the glory of heaven."[5]

The Interior Castle teaches us that the Christian life is a journey of deepening intimacy with Christ through surrender and prayer. Relationship with the Lord deepens as prayer moves from casual conversation (friendship) to interior communion (courtship) to intimate contemplation (marriage). On this extraordinary journey a spiritual director is God's gracious gift for facilitating the pilgrim's growth in Christ.

The Puritan Model: Combating Sin

THE PILGRIM'S PROGRESS, by John Bunyan (d. 1688), is the most popular work of Christian spirituality in the English language. The allegory traces Christian's challenging journey from the City of Destruction to the Celestial City. Beginning the journey, Christian and a copilgrim, Pliable, come to the Slough of Despond, where they wallow in difficulties. Disheartened by the troubles, Pliable abandons the journey and is seen no more. Proceeding alone, Christian climbs the Hill of Difficulty on his knees, passes through the Valley of Humiliation, and then through the Valley of the Shadow of Death—a desolate place full of dangers. Christian encounters many unnecessary trials because he journeys alone. When Christian joins up with Faithful in the wilderness he finds a supportive soul mate for the journey.

The pair pass through Vanity Fair, presided over by demons:

> At this fair all kinds of things were sold, such as houses, lands, trades, professions, places, honors . . . lusts, pleasures and delights of all sorts,—such as prostitutes, wives, husbands, children, masters, servants, lives, blood, bodies, souls, silver, gold, pearls, precious stones and what not. At this fair there is at all times to be seen juggling, cheats, games, plays, fools, mimics, knaves, and rogues of every kind. Here are to be seen, too, thefts, murders, adulteries, false swearers, and obscenities of all kinds.[6]

Christian and Faithful were cast into prison in the town because of their testimony; soon thereafter Faithful was killed by the devilish authorities.

Christian is joined by another pilgrim, Hopeful, and the two sleep on the grounds of Doubting Castle. The owner, Great Despair, throws them into a dark dungeon and beats them mercilessly. The pair move on to Delectable Mountain, where they meet shepherds who feed them, care for their wounds, and point them to the Celestial City. Companions on the perilous journey, Christian and Hopeful share their stories and sing songs to each other.

Along the Way the pilgrims encounter many surly characters who strive to deflect them from their goal. The names of the false counselors betray their subtle temptations: Worldly Wisdom, Wanton, Legality, Vain-Confidence, Flatterer, and Atheist. Chief of the adversaries is deceiving

Apollyon, who tries to lure them to his own destructive place.

Helpful counselors come alongside Christian and his friends. Evangelist points them to the wicket gate that leads to Mount Zion; the King of the Celestial City commissions Goodwill to be Christian's guide along the Way; and a helper named Interpreter expounds the whole counsel of God to the weary pilgrims.

Christian and Hopeful pass through Enchanted Ground and enter the country of Beulah, on the border of heaven. From there they catch a glimpse of the Celestial City arrayed in awesome splendor. But first they must cross the formidable River of Death. With their eyes fixed on Jesus on the other side, together they ford the river and climb the hill to Jerusalem on high. The King joyously welcomes them home, and upon each of their heads is placed a crown of gold. Joined by the angelic host and the saints of all ages, Christian and Hopeful worship and praise the King forever.

Bunyan's allegory describes the temptations, discouragements, and hostile powers pilgrims encounter on the homeward journey. Emphasizing the temptations we face, it may saddle us with a sin focus that leaves God at a distance. A welcome feature of Bunyan's allegory is the counselors, the spiritual guides, who keep the pilgrims focused on the path to the Celestial City.

Notes

Chapter 1

1. Lauren F. Winner, "From Mass Evangelist to Soul Friend," *Christianity Today,* 2 October 2000, p. 58.
2. Bernard of Clairvaux, as quoted by G. McLeod Bryan, *In His Likeness* (Louisville, John Knox Press, 1959), p. 46.
3. Clement of Alexandria, "Who Is the Rich Man That Shall be Saved?" in *Ante-Nicene Fathers,* vol. 2 (Peabody, Mass.: Hendrickson, 1994), p. 21.
4. Gregory the Great, as quoted by Bryan, p. 42.
5. Thomas à Kempis, *The Imitation of Christ*, ed. Donald E. Demaray (Grand Rapids: Baker Books, 1982), p. 11.
6. John Arndt, as quoted by Bryan, p. 117.
7. François Fénelon, *Christian Perfection* (New York: Harper, 1947), p. 43.
8. John Calvin, *Institutes of the Christian Religion*, IV.19.29, Library of Christian Classics, vol. XXI (Philadelphia: Westminster Press, 1960), p. 1477.
9. William Law, as quoted by Bryan, p. 139.

Chapter 2

1. George Gallup, Jr. and Timothy Jones, *The Next American Spirituality* (Colorado Springs: Victor Books, 2000), pp. 177, 178, 180.
2. Jamling Tenzing Norgay, *Touching My Father's Soul* (San Francisco: HarperSanFrancisco, 2001), p. 198.
3. George Barna and Mark Hatch, *Boiling Point* (Ventura, Calif.: Regal Books, 2001), p. 186.
4. *USA TODAY*, 27 June 2001, p. 7D.
5. Barna and Hatch, p. 223.
6. Composed by George Carlin and transmitted via e-mail by a third party.
7. Barna Research Online, "America is Spiritually Stagnant," www.barna.org, accessed March 5, 2001.
8. Reported in *Ministries Today*, May/June 2000, p. 23.
9. Barna and Hatch, p. 225.

10. Reported in *The Dallas Evening News*, 25 December 1998.
11. "Families Unite in Grief Over Slayings," *Denver Post*, 8 April 2001, p. 1B.
12. Years ago Henry David Thoreau observed, "The mass of men [and women] lead lives of quiet desperation." *Walden, or Life in the Woods* (New York: Libra Collection, 1960), p. 7.
13. "Clergy Concerns," *In Trust* (2001), p. 25.
14. Adrian van Kaam, *Looking for Jesus* (Denneville, N.J.: Dimension Books, 1978), p. 63.

Chapter 3
1. Larry Crabb, *The Safest Place on Earth* (Nashville: Word, 1999), p. 182.
2. Augustine, *Christian Instruction*, I.34, in *The Fathers of the Church*, vol. 4 (Washington, D.C.: Catholic University Press, 1950), p. 55.
3. Irenaeus, *Against Heresies*, IV.11.1, in *Ante Nicene Fathers*, vol. 1 (Grand Rapids: Eerdmans, 1981), p. 474.
4. Lee B. Spitzer, *Endless Possibilities* (Lincoln: Spiritual Journey Press, 1997), pp. 40-42.
5. Gregory of Nyssa, *The Life of Moses, The Classics of Western Christian Spirituality* (New York: Paulist Press, 1978), pp. 37-51.
6. Janet O. Hagberg and Robert Guelich, *The Critical Journey: Stages in the Life of Faith* (Salem, Wis.: Sheffield, 1995).
7. Hagberg and Guelich, pp. 93-94.
8. Hagberg and Guelich, p. 137.
9. Hagberg and Guelich, p. 153.
10. Thomas à Kempis, *The Imitation of Christ*, ed. Donald E. Demaray (Grand Rapids: Baker Books, 1982), p. 76.
11. M. Scott Peck, *The Different Drum* (New York: Simon and Schuster, 1987), p. 195.
12. Walter Brueggemann, *Praying the Psalms* (Winona, Minn.: Saint Mary's Press, 1982), pp. 16-23.

Chapter 4
1. "Saga of Terminal Illness Tests 'Dateline' Producer," *USA TODAY*, 23 December 1999, p. 4D.
2. Dallas Willard, "Spiritual Formation—Why Bother?" www.forministry.com, accessed July 10, 2001.
3. Bobb Biehl, *Mentoring: Confidence in Finding a Mentor and Becoming One* (Nashville: Broadman & Holman, 1996), p. 30.
4. Richard V. Peace, "From Discipleship to Spiritual Direction," *Theology News and Notes*, March 1999, p. 7.

5. "What Is Mentoring?" The Uncommon Individual Foundation, www.mentoringfoundation.org, accessed July 5, 2001.
6. Biehl, p. 30.
7. Fred Smith, "Mentoring That Matters," *Leadership Journal,* Winter 1999, p. 95.
8. Simon Chan, *Spiritual Theology* (Downers Grove, Ill.: InterVarsity, 1998), p. 226.
9. Stephen Strang, "Don't Struggle Alone," *Ministries Today,* November/December 2000, p. 38.
10. Henri Nouwen, "Spiritual Direction," *Worship* 55, 1981, p. 402.
11. Larry Crabb, *The Safest Place on Earth* (Nashville: Word, 1999), p. 181.
12. G. Campbell Morgan, *The Gospel According to John* (London: Marshall, Morgan & Scott, 1933), p. 46.

Chapter 5
1. *The Sayings of the Desert Fathers*, trans. Benedicta Ward (Kalamazoo, Mich.: Cistercian Publications, 1984), p. xxvi.
2. *The Sayings of the Desert Fathers,* p. 154.
3. Basil, as quoted by Kenneth Leech in *Soul Friend* (New York: Harper, 1977), p. 41.
4. Gordon S. Jackson, *Quotes for the Journey* (Colorado Springs: NavPress, 2000), p. 133.
5. Gregory, *Pastoral Rule*, I.1, in *The Nicene and Post-Nicene Fathers*, second series, vol. 12 (Grand Rapids: Eerdmans, 1979), p 1.
6. Bernard of Clairvaux, as quoted by Tilden Edwards in *Spiritual Friend* (New York: Paulist, 1980), p. 248.
7. Aelred, as quoted by Leech, p. 54.
8. Thomas à Kempis, *The Imitation of Christ*, ed. Donald E. Demaray (Grand Rapids: Baker Books, 1982), p. 18.
9. Teresa of Avila, *The Book of Her Life*, 19.15, in *The Collected Works of St. Teresa of Avila*, vol. 1, trans. Kiernan Kavanaugh and Otilio Rodriguez (Washington, D.C.: ICS Publications, 1976), p. 128.
10. Teresa of Avila, *Autobiography*, trans. David Love (Westminster, Md.: Newman Press, 1962), p. 104.
11. John of the Cross, *The Ascent of Mount Carmel*, Prologue, in *The Collected Works of St. John of the Cross*, trans. Kavanaugh and Rodriguez (Washington, D.C.: ICS Publications, 1973), p. 70.
12. Francis of Sales, *Introduction to the Devout Life*, I.4, (Westminster, M.D.: Newman Press, 1956), pp. 15-16.
13. Jeremy Taylor, as quoted by Reginald Somerset Ward in *A Guide for Spiritual Directors* (London: A.R. Mowbray, 1958), p. 9.

14. Richard Baxter, *The Reformed Pastor*, ed. James M. Houston (Portland: Multnomah Press, 1982), pp. 73-78.

15. François Fénelon, *Talking With God*, ed. Hal M. Helms (Brewster, Mass.: Paraclete Press, 1997), contains fifty-one of his letters.

16. Reginald Somerset Ward, p. 8.

17. C. S. Lewis, as quoted by Paul Clasper in "C. S. Lewis as Spiritual Director," *Review for Religious* 48.2, March/April 1989, p. 272.

18. Thomas Merton, *Spiritual Direction and Meditation* (Collegeville, Minn.: Liturgical Press, 1960), p. 9.

19. Eugene Peterson, *Working the Angles* (Grand Rapids: Eerdmans, 1987), p. 121.

20. Peterson, p. 107.

21. Henri Nouwen, *The Living Reminder* (Minneapolis: Seabury Press, 1977), p. 72.

22. "Pastor's Progress," *Leadership,* Fall 2000, pp. 24-31.

23. Thomas Oden, *Care of Souls in the Classic Tradition* (Philadelphia: Fortress Press, 1984), p. 39.

Chapter 6

1. Roy Lessin, as quoted in *Quotes for the Journey*, compiled by Gordon S. Jackson (Colorado Springs: NavPress 2000), p. 174.

Chapter 7

1. Quoted by Alfred Plummer, *The Gospel According to Luke* (Grand Rapids: Baker Books, 1981), p. 122.

2. John Calvin, *Commentary on the Gospel According to John,* vol.1 (Grand Rapids: Eerdmans, 1956), p. 152.

3. Ephraem, as quoted by George R. Beasley-Murray, *John. Word Biblical Commentary* (Nashville: Word, 1987), p. 66.

4. John Bosco, as quoted by Ronda De Sola Chervin, *Quotable Saints* (Ann Arbor: Servant Publications, 1992), p. 25.

5. Janet K. Ruffing, *Spiritual Direction* (New York: Paulist Press, 2000), p. 35.

6. William A. Barry and William J. Connolly, *The Practice of Spiritual Direction* (San Francisco: HarperSanFrancisco, 1982), p. 89.

Chapter 8

1. Brooke Foss Westcott, *The Gospel According to St. John* (1980; reprint, Grand Rapids: Baker Books), p. 183.

2. G. Campbell Morgan, *The Gospel According to John* (London: Marshall, Morgan & Scott, 1933), p. 88.

3. Josef Pieper, *Faith, Hope, Love* (Ft. Collins, Colo.: Ignatius, 1997), p. 118.

4. Kenneth Boa, *Conformed to His Image* (Grand Rapids: Zondervan, 2001), p. 192.

5. James Stalker, *The Seven Deadly Sins* (Colorado Springs: NavPress, 1998), p. 77.

6. John Cassian, *Conferences. Ancient Christian Writers* series, vol. 57 (New York: Paulist Press, 1997), p. 189.

Chapter 9

1. Gerald May, *Care of Mind, Care of Spirit* (San Francisco: HarperSanFrancisco, 1992), p. 46.

2. C. H. Spurgeon, *Popular Exposition of Matthew* (Grand Rapids: Zondervan, 1962), p. 141.

3. John of the Cross, as quoted by Susan Muto, *Dear Master* (Liguori, Mo.: Liguori/Triumph, 1999), p. xix.

4. William Barclay, *The Gospel of Matthew*, vol. 2 (Philadelphia: Westminster Press, 1958), p. 180.

5. Alan H. McNeile, *The Gospel According to Matthew* (1980; reprint, Grand Rapids: Baker Books), p. 250.

Chapter 10

1. This story is not found in the earliest and most reliable manuscripts of John's gospel. Scribes who copied the Gospels were uncertain as to its exact location, hence its appearance at various places in manuscripts of John as well as in the gospel of Luke. There is little doubt that this story is a genuine incident in the ministry of Jesus.

2. Augustine, *Homilies on the Gospel of John*, vol. 1 (Grand Rapids: Eerdmans, 1983), p. 198.

3. William Barclay, *The Gospel of John*, vol. 2 (Philadelphia: Westminster Press, 1956), p. 9.

4. T. W. Manson, *Jesus and the Non-Jews* (London: Athlone Press, 1955), p. 10.

5. C. S. Lewis, *Letters to an American Lady* (Grand Rapids: Eerdmans, 1967), p. 77.

6. Henri Nouwen, *Return of the Prodigal Son* (New York: Image Books, 1993), p. 53.

7. C. S. Lewis, *Letters: C.S. Lewis/Don Giovanni Calabria* (Ann Arbor: Servant Publications, 1988), p. 67

8. Thelma Hall, *Too Deep for Words* (New York: Paulist Press, 1988), p. 54.

Chapter 11

1. "Balance Body and Soul," *USA TODAY,* 7 September 2001, p. 3D.
2. George Barna and Mark Hatch, *Boiling Point* (Ventura, Calif.: Regal Books, 2001), p. 101.
3. Thomas Merton, *New Seeds of Contemplation* (Norfolk, Conn.: New Directions, 1962), p. 19.
4. *Great Devotional Classics: Selections from the Writings of Evelyn Underhill,* ed. Douglas Steere (Nashville: The Upper Room, 1961), p. 10.
5. A. W. Tozer, *The Pursuit of God* (Camp Hill, Pa.: Christian Publications, 1982), pp. 96-97.

Chapter 12

1. C. S. Lewis, *Mere Christianity* (London: Geoffrey Bles, 1952), p. 168.
2. Augustine, as quoted by Jill Haak Adels in *The Wisdom of the Saints* (New York: Oxford University Press, 1987), p. 164.
3. Augustine, *Sermon,* 311.15, in *The Works of St. Augustine,* part 3, vol. 9 (Hyde Park, N.Y.: New York City Press, 1994), p. 78.
4. Augustine, *The Trinity,* 2.17, in *The Fathers of the Church,* vol. 45 (Washington, D.C.: Catholic University of America Press, 1963), p. 86.
5. John Wesley, as quoted by Gordon S. Jackson in *Quotes for the Journey* (Colorado Springs: NavPress, 2000), p. 110.
6. Augustine, *Letter,* 31.5., in *The Fathers of the Church,* vol. 12 (Washington, D.C.: Catholic University of America Press, 1951), p. 115.
7. Athanasius, *Life of Antony,* 17, in *Nicene and Post-Nicene Fathers,* second series, vol. 4 (Grand Rapids: Eerdmans, 1980), pp. 200-201.

Chapter 13

1. Chrysostom, *Epistle to the Romans,* homily 18 (Grand Rapids: Eerdmans, 1979), p. 483.

Chapter 14

1. Augustine, *The Gospel According to St. John,* vol. 2 (Grand Rapids: Eerdmans, 1978), p. 314.
2. Jane Greer and Margery Rosen, *How Could You Do This to Me?* (New York: Doubleday, 1997), p. 12.
3. James Stalker, *The Life of Jesus Christ* (New York: American Tract Society, 1891), p. 119.

Chapter 15

1. Adapted from an actual life story by Doug Herman in *Faith Quake* (Grand Rapids: Baker Books, 2002). Used with permission.
2. Adrian Van Kaam, *Looking for Jesus* (Denneville, N.J.: Dimension Books, 1978), p. 113.
3. R. Kent Hughes, *John* (Wheaton, Ill.: Crossway, 1999), p. 355.
4. C. S. Lewis, *The World's Last Night* (New York: Harcourt Brace, 1959), p. 8.
5. Van Kaam, p. 134.

Chapter 16

1. Augustine, *Homilies on the Gospel of John,* vol. 2 (Grand Rapids: Eerdmans, 1978), p. 241.
2. Henri Nouwen, *Return of the Prodigal Son* (New York: Image Books, 1993), p. 121.
3. Henri Nouwen, *Lifesigns* (New York: Doubleday, 1986), p. 38.
4. Augustine, *Expositions on the Psalms* (Grand Rapids: Eerdmans, 1983), p. 69.

Chapter 17

1. David E. Rosage, *Beginning Spiritual Direction* (Ann Arbor: Servant Publications, 1994), p. 48.
2. W. H. G. Thomas, *Outline Studies in the Gospel of Luke* (Grand Rapids: Eerdmans, 1950), p. 377.
3. Martin Luther, as quoted by Mary Louise Bringle, *Despair: Sickness or Sin?* (Nashville: Abingdon, 1990), p. 59.
4. Martin Luther, as quoted by Bringle, p. 151.
5. George Gallup, Jr. and Timothy Jones, *The New American Spirituality* (Colorado Springs: Victor Books, 2000), pp. 185-186.

Chapter 18

1. Many commentators on John's gospel (Westcott, Plummer, G. C. Morgan, Robertson, Temple, Hobbs, Guthrie, Laney) believe that Jesus intentionally made a distinction between *agapō* and *phileō* to bring to Peter's consciousness the shallowness of his love. So also the *Life Application Study Bible,* p. 2286 and *The NIV Study Bible,* p. 1638. Nowhere in Scripture are we commanded to love God or others with *philia*—always with *agapē*.

Other commentators (Tasker, Beasley-Murray, Morris, Carson, Burge) judge that Jesus' use of the two words for "love" is merely stylistic.

2. F. F. Bruce, *The Gospel of John* (Grand Rapids: Eerdmans, 1983), p. 405.

3. Adrian van Kaam, *Looking for Jesus* (Rockaway, N.J.: Dimension Books, 1978), p. 50.

4. Van Kaam, p. 48.

5. *Life Application Study Bible* (Wheaton, Ill.: Tyndale House; Grand Rapids: Zondervan, 1995), p. 2033.

6. From stanza three of the hymn, "Come Thou Fount of Every Blessing," by Robert Robinson.

Chapter 19

1. W. M. Ramsey, *The Church in the Roman Empire* (Grand Rapids: Baker Books, 1954), p. 32.

2. Basil, as quoted by Ronda De Sola Chervin in *Quotable Saints* (Ann Arbor: Servant Publications, 1992), p. 16.

3. Abba Agathon, as quoted by Roger Ray in *Christian Wisdom for Today* (St. Louis: Chalice, 1999), pp. 68-69.

4. Jerome, as quoted by De Sola Chervin, p. 168.

5. Adapted from Gary Collins, *Christian Counseling* (Nashville: Word, 1988), p. 109.

6. Neil T. Anderson, et al., *Christ Centered Therapy* (Grand Rapids: Zondervan, 2000), p. 156.

Chapter 20

1. F. B. Meyer, *Gospel of John* (Washington, Pa.: Christian Literature Crusade, 1970), p. 115.

2. Reginald H. Fuller, *Interpreting the Miracles* (Philadelphia: Westminster Press, 1963), p. 107.

Chapter 21

1. Augustine, *Homilies on the Gospel of St. John* (Grand Rapids: Eerdmans, 1983), p. 396.

2. David G. Benner, *Care of Souls* (Grand Rapids: Baker Books, 1998), p. 131.

Chapter 22

1. William L. Lane, *The Gospel of Mark* (London: Marshall, Morgan & Scott, 1974), p. 516.

2. Dale Bruner, *Matthew*, vol. 2 (Nashville: Word, 1990), p. 983, writes: Jesus "does not seek to disobey the will of God, but longs that God's will might be different."

3. See Bruner, vol. 2, p. 988.
4. Lane, p. 518.

Chapter 23
1. Herschel H. Hobbs, *The Gospel of Mark* (Grand Rapids: Baker Books, 1970), p. 248.

Chapter 24
1. Dietrich Bonhoeffer, *Life Together* (San Francisco: HarperSanFrancisco, 1976), p. 97.
2. A. W. Tozer, *Of God and Men* (Camp Hill, Pa.: Christian Publications, 1960), p. 67.
3. Gerald May, *Care of Mind, Care of Spirit* (San Francisco: Harper San Francisco, 1992), pp. 210-211.
4. Katherine Hanley, "Jesus as Spiritual Director," *Spiritual Life* 31.2, Summer 1985, p. 77.
5. David Benner, *Care of Souls* (Grand Rapids: Baker Books, 1998), p. 28.

Chapter 25
1. Teresa of Avila, *Interior Castle*, mansion 6, trans. E. Allison Peers (New York: Doubleday; New York: Image, 1961), p. 183.
2. *Songs and Prayers for Taizé,* (Chicago: GIA Publications, 1996), p. 49.
3. Paul J. Roy, "Inside Out: Spiritual Direction for Ministry," *Journal of Pastoral Care* 22.1, 1987, p. 11.
4. Henri Nouwen, *The Wounded Healer: Ministry in Contemporary Society* (New York: Doubleday, 1972).

Epilogue
1. Thomas Green, *Weeds Among the Wheat* (Notre Dame, Ind.: Ave Maria, 1984), p. 79.
2. http://www.sdiworld.org.
3. Teresa of Avila, as quoted by Tilden Edwards in *Spiritual Friend* (New York: Paulist Press, 1980), p. 250.

Appendix
1. Bernard of Clairvaux, *On Loving God*, in *Bernard of Clairvaux: Selected Writings*, trans. G. R. Evans, *The Classics of Western Spirituality* (New York: Paulist Press, 1987), pp. 173-205.
2. Richard Sibbes, *Works, The Soul's Conflict*, vol. 1 (London: J. Nichol, 1862), p. 247.

3. Teresa of Avila, *The Classics of Western Spirituality, The Interior Castle* (New York: Paulist Press, 1979), p. 44.
4. Teresa of Avila, p. 126.
5. Teresa of Avila, p. 178.
6. John Bunyan, *The Pilgrim's Progress* (Brewster, Mass.: Paraclete Press, 1982), p. 151.

About the Author

DR. BRUCE DEMAREST is a professor at Denver Seminary and the author of ten books, including *Satisfy Your Soul* (NavPress), *Integrative Theology* (Zondervan), and *The Cross and Salvation* (Crossway). He is a graduate of Wheaton College and Trinity Evangelical Divinity School. Dr. Demarest earned his doctorate in biblical and historical theology at the University of Manchester, where he was mentored by Professor F. F. Bruce.